From Fright to Fight to Farm
A Journey of Survival

Ernest Kaufman

DENVER, COLORADO

Outskirts Press, Inc.
http://www.outskirtspress.com

ISBN: 978-1-4787-6869-2

Outskirts Press and the "OP" logo are trademarks belonging to Outskirts Press, Inc.

PRINTED IN THE UNITED STATES OF AMERICA

This book is dedicated to the memory of my wonderful parents, whose lives were so prematurely ended by the Holocaust

Table of Contents

Acknowledgements

Nancy Nilsson was interviewing my wife Mina for a story about her life when I arrived on the scene, and when Nancy heard what I could contribute to her story and how much I was part of Mina's life, she decided to make Mina's story a part of my life story instead.

Based on my memory, along with documents, photos, newspaper articles, magazine stories and records of my military service, Nancy was able to write a most comprehensive story of a rather unusual life that spanned more than eighty years. When, for personal reasons, she was unable to finish it after she had written a large part of my story, I sat down at my computer and finished the book, changing Nancy's third person writing into first person format with virtually no change in content.

Joanne Thomas is an excellent editor and a stickler for accuracy. She carefully edited what Nancy and I had written and made some very useful suggestions that we were glad to accept.

I am forever grateful to Nancy and Joanne, two dear friends, who spent so much of their time and effort (and at arguments with me) until we finished my Journey of Survival story.

Preface

At a monthly meeting of the Fort Dix, NJ chapter of the Retired Officers Association, US Navy Captain John Ingraham detected a slight foreign accent in my speech and asked me about my background. After a lengthy conversation, he emphatically said: "Ernest, you must tell your story, because many people have no idea of the effect the Holocaust had on individual families or survivors, and especially what you personally went through. And, you might as well start here, with a talk to our members!"

With the exception of family and friends, I had never spoken publicly about my life experiences and I was surprised when, after I spoke to our chapter members at a meeting several weeks later, I was asked by several of them to tell my story to other organizations of which they were members. After that I spoke at churches, synagogues, veterans groups, senior citizens groups, Rotary clubs and other civic organizations; I also spoke at Holocaust Remembrance Services at Fort Dix and other military installations, and I found that most inquisitive of all my audiences were the students I spoke to at public schools.

I became a volunteer at the Holocaust Education Center of the Jewish Community Center in Cherry Hill, NJ, and over more than twelve years I have told my story to several thousand school children of various ages. Their questions were unending. They covered my early years, my family history, the Holocaust period, my war time experiences and other pursuits so thoroughly that it made me realize that I somehow had to tell my story in as much detail as I possibly could.

Needless to say, many of the questions posed by the students could not be answered in the short time allotted to a speaking engagement that was followed by a brief question and answer period. At a time when it seemed that interest in the lessons the Holocaust taught us was beginning to diminish, and the number of survivors and of World War II veterans who can give live testimony to it is shrinking daily, I felt it was more important than ever to do whatever else I could to keep the memory alive, particularly in the minds of so many young people, so that they might be instrumental in keeping it from becoming just a footnote in history.

At that point, the rest of my story just seemed to develop once I knew that a nascent curiosity needed to be satisfied, and I then decided to share the rest of my life story—my service in the American Army and my life as a poultry farmer—two completely different, unrelated careers that spanned more than forty years.

Although retired by now, and in addition to this book, I'll also continue to tell my "From Fright to Fight to Farm" story to any individual or group willing to hear me speak as long as I am able to do so.

1.

Beginnings

IN THE EARLY 1930s, before many public records were destroyed by the bombing and fighting during WW II, my cousin Kurt Steinberg, who had grown up in Altenessen, a suburb of Essen in Germany, began gathering information about the Kaufmann's extended family. By tracking down local census files, synagogue and church records, studying headstones, and calling on stories drawn from family members and personal memory, Kurt was able to compile a remarkably thorough record of the Kaufmanns. Thanks to him, and to others for adding more details and clarifications, an extensive Kaufmann family tree dating back to 1712 now exists. Additionally, a book titled *Life and Loss in the Shadow of the Holocaust* by Rebecca Boehling and Uta Larkey that chronicles other members of our family was published in 2011 by Cambridge University Press. Together with this account, the story of a family with remarkable strength, character, and resilience has emerged.

From the start, this could not have been an easy process. When Kurt began his research, there were no data bases, search engines or computers. The information was gathered painstakingly over a period of several years. Tracing Jewish ancestry in particular presented some unique hurdles since, for centuries, Jews were driven from one place to another, often excluded from the privileges of citizenry, and disenfranchised from the larger communities in which they lived. For more years than not in the last millennium they were not allowed to own land, to enroll in most public schools and universities, to hold certain professions, or to work in trades and businesses. Thus, data concerning people that might have otherwise been found in school enrollment records and class rosters, land sales, title documents or business ledgers often did not exist if these people happened to be Jews.

Complicating research further was the fact that prior to the 1700s Jews did not, as an existing rule, have surnames. While designations to distinguish one person from another fairly well developed during the Middle Ages, they tended to be patronymic, such as David ben Yacob (David, son of Jacob), by birthplace or adult residence (R. Jerhiel of Paris), or - in rare instances - by title and acronym, as was the case with the renowned Rabbi Moses b. Maimon who became known as RaMBaM. However, by the 1700s Jews had settled into the practice of either creating a surname which identified them with the region in which they lived, or by their profession, or by accepting a name that was forced on them by others. Whichever of these was the case, my first documented ancestor, as Kurt discovered from records he found, was a maternal great-great grandfather known as Levi, whose family name became "Schwarz." Levi was born in 1712 (died in 1805) and lived with his wife Theodora in Luexheim, a village south of Cologne and Aachen, near the western border of Germany. Their son Joseph and his wife Jeanette's daughter Blandine (Taeubchen) in 1814 married into the Kaufmann family. One of her and her husband Jacob Kaufmann's eight children was Isaak, my grandfather. My paternal great-great grandfather was a man named Simon who was born in the 1740s in Wallertheim, in Hesse, and died in 1828 in Schiefbahn, where he had settled with his wife Sara. He and his son Jacob, who became the husband of Taeubchen Schwarz, took the name of "Kaufmann." The German word for businessman, merchant or tradesman is *Kaufmann*, and this in all likelihood provides a clue to Jacob's livelihood as well as permanently becoming the family surname. (When I applied for a Green Card upon my arrival in the United States, I changed my name from "Ernst Kaufmann" to "Ernest Kaufman," and both names are used here interchangeably).

Much beyond names, dates, and places of residence, there is little detailed information about the Kaufmann family until the mid-1800s, when the ancestral tree "blossoms" with my paternal grandparents, Isaak and Caroline Kaufmann, nee Cappel (born in Wassenberg, a town on the Roer River, near the Dutch border). From then to the present, the family's story gains depth and breadth with historical records, photographs, family anecdotes, and my own personal memories. It is with Isaak and Caroline that my story really begins.

2.

The Kaufmanns and the Roers

ISAAC (1824-1886) AND Caroline Kaufmann (1843-1887) lived in the German town of Schiefbahn. In records that date back to the 1300s, Schiefbahn is referred to in passing as a "village." However, by 1430 it had grown into a well-established, flourishing town due in no small part to its strategic location on a road that ran between the Rhine and Meuse Rivers.

By 1814 Schiefbahn was known as a textile center, and it was also when a "Jewish Community" numbering fifty individuals was identified in the town's records. A synagogue that was built in Schiefbahn in 1854 was renovated in 1890. It is here in Schiefbahn where a clear history of the Kaufmann family emerges with my grandparents, Isaak and Caroline.

Isaak was a highly respected businessman, who dealt primarily with horses used not only for farm and carriage work, but also for pulling boats and barges along rivers and canals. This meant a lot of travel, primarily to Belgium. He was very religious, learned and exceptionally knowledgeable about Judaica. He also had an impressive Hebrew book collection. Caroline was described as a beautiful woman, blond, and having "clear and pure lines and big eyes." Despite the big difference in age, the marriage was an extremely happy one, and their children often remarked that "We never heard a harsh word exchanged between them."

Isaak and Caroline Kaufmann had eleven children; they were Julie, Gustav, Bertha, Selma, Amalie, Emma, Henriette, Paula, Leo, Siegfried and Thekla. Among Jews, large families were commonplace, and extended families lived in relatively close proximity to one another. Because of worship practices, holiday celebrations and dietary restrictions, as well as shared customs and culture, an intrinsically tightly-knit Jewish community formed whose members all knew of, and cared for each other. Thus, when both Caroline and Isaak died (he from injuries sustained supposedly after being kicked by a horse; she from acute appendicitis) and their oldest child was barely eighteen, all their children were taken into the homes of various relatives. Gustav and Amalie had died as infants, and Siegfried, until he died at age 14 and the other eight children were raised within a protective circle of extended family. While the loss of their parents was certainly profound, the Kaufmann siblings were able to live near, and stay in close contact with each other.

Isaak and Caroline's only surviving son, Leo, was taken in by Isaak's second cousin Leopold Kaufmann and his wife Johanna, or Hannchen, as she was called. Uncle Leopold and Aunt Hannchen lived in the village of Drove, where they owned a butcher shop. They had no children of their own, and young Leo could not have been more loved or cared for had he been Leopold and Hannchen's own son.

Had his parents not died before he was grown and given a choice, Leo probably would have attended university and become an architect, a desire he later often expressed to his own two children. However, with the changed circumstances of his life that dream was set aside, and Leo was expected to join Uncle Leopold in his business, and to eventually take it over. Thus it was, as the 1800s drew to a close that Leo, in his early twenties by then, and having returned from his two years of compulsory military service, probably spent his days working with his uncle in the butcher shop, studying to become a "shochet" (one who does the ritual slaughter of animals), attending synagogue, studying Torah, and celebrating the Sabbath and holidays with the small Jewish community. In due course, Leo Kaufmann would become my father.

About this same time, in the village of Buir, about fifteen miles from Drove, another couple—Gustav and Caroline Roer—was also raising a family. Because it was not uncommon for cousins to marry cousins—and religious Jews only married other Jews at that time—the branches of the Kaufmann and Roer families had occasion to intertwine more than once over the years. For instance, Uncle Leopold Kaufman and Caroline (Kaufmann) Roer were second cousins. Aunt Hannchen (Roer) Kaufmann and Gustav Roer were brother and sister.

Gustav and Caroline Roer had five children. There was Fritz, who in 1918 was killed in action in WWI, and Felix, who died in 1923 of injuries sustained while in the German army during the war. Son Joseph was born in 1885, and then came Karl, in 1886. The Roer's last child and only daughter, Else was born on August 25, 1890. Having attended a then very popular "Finishing School," this pretty girl became a quiet and gentle young woman who would, in time, become my mother.

My parents most likely knew each other since childhood because of the close connection and interrelations between the two families, and it was to no one's surprise that Leo fell in love with the pretty young girl twelve years his junior. He courted her and married her on February 1, 1914. In a "roasting" at their wedding, one of the speakers proclaimed that "For the seventh time a Kaufmann is diving into the Roer," to much applause; Roer was a nearby river "Rur's" Dutch name that had been my mother's family's surname.

At the time Else and Leo started life together, Else's father Gustav was the owner of a well-established plumbing, heating, and roofing company. Despite the unwritten practice of the governing authorities to keep Jews out of government contracts, Gustav's work ethic and product gained him the reputation and respect of even his toughest non-Jewish competitors, and while other Jewish tradesmen were denied contracts, or were simply never issued work permits, Gustav Roer's track record for excellence and integrity were so well known that he could not be denied, and he is believed to have been the first Jew in the county to be awarded contracts for work on county buildings and other public institutions in the area. His business grew to where at times he had more than 20 men in his employ.

In addition to Gustav's plumbing business, the Roers owned a household goods and appliance store that was managed and run by Caroline (both of my grandmothers were named "Caroline"). I recall my Grandmother Roer's store fondly. Its inventory included everything from bicycles to bathtubs, pots and pans, and the stoves to put them on. The store was not only a favorite spot for local women to shop, but also the place to linger for gossiping and exchanging of neighborhood news. Both Grandfather Gustav's plumbing shop and Grandmother Caroline's store were favorite haunts for me, who—as a boy—found no end to the interesting corners and items to explore, plus the likelihood of going home with some sort of treat from a store shelf. Watching men in the shop repair or put together what they needed before they left for their jobs, or looking at the many things in the supply room, or going to the garden to look at grandfather's pride, a bed of beautiful flowers that he planted every year, were things I always loved to do whenever I visited.

The Roers were hardworking people, successful in business; dutiful to tradition and family. But, while prosperous, life was anything but easy. My grandparents were to lose three of their five children within their own lifetime—sons Felix and Fritz during or because of World War I, and then 42 year old Karl, who was active in their business, in a streetcar accident in 1928. He left behind a young wife and two young sons whom my grandparents supported, and then groomed them to take over the family business. Their son Joseph died in 1942 in Gurs, an Internment Camp in southern France.

During their engagement, my father had a house built where he and his bride would live, directly across the street from Uncle Leopold and Aunt Hannchen's house and butcher shop. The young couple not only started married life with a new house, conveniently located close to family and father's work, and — thanks to mother's father, Gustav—one that was reported to have been among the first homes in Drove with indoor plumbing, a flush toilet, a porcelain bathtub and a coal-fired heater next to it to provide the unheard-of luxury of a hot bath…all indoors!

The young bride and groom had a sweet, if all too short few months together, when in July of 1914 World War I had been declared. Father had already served his compulsory two-year term in the German army, from 1898 to 1900, and undoubtedly believed he had satisfied his military obligation. Unfortunately, this was not to be the case, and—at thirty-six years old—he was called up for wartime service. Mother, who was newly pregnant with their first child, did not want to live alone. She moved back to her parents' home in Buir and surrendered their new home in Drove to a tenant until my father returned to be with her again. Much as he hated to go to war, my father did his duty fighting for his country during WWI, and he was fortunate to escape physical and mental injuries during the four years he wore his country's military uniform. My mother gave birth to a healthy baby girl, Lotte, on November 9, 1914, and father, whenever he had leave, would spend all his time with his young family in Buir. The war ended in 1918, more than four years after it had begun, and, decorated with the Iron Cross, Master Sargent Leo Kaufmann returned home.

Else and Leo promptly moved back to their home in Drove. Four-year-old Lotte came to realize that Leo was "Daddy" who lived with them all the time now, and not just the "Uncle Daddy" who always visited them for a short time, only to have to leave again. Uncle Leopold died shortly after my father had returned and resumed work in the butcher shop, while mother tended their house, the gardens and her toddler. Life returned to its normal routine, and then, on June 7, 1920—the same year that marked the beginning of horrible inflation in Germany—the Kaufmanns were blessed with me, their second child.

3.

Germany after World War I

IN THE MIDST of these difficult times, our family managed to get by easier than many families, especially those living in the cities. We Kaufmanns had several advantages that allowed us to continue to live fairly comfortably. We lived in the country, in a largely self-sustaining lifestyle rather than in the city, where most daily needs were purchased and not produced, and shortages were often felt more acutely. The Kaufmann family owned its own homes and business. It had several parcels of pasture land for its milk cows and their horse; gardens and fruit trees, and chickens that gave us eggs. Our father was a butcher, a profession that provided a necessary service to the local community while also putting meat on his own family's table.

Still, we were not exempt from the effects of French occupation. I vividly remember that French Foreign Legion troops were quartered in barracks on the outskirts of Drove, and that all the officers were white and the troops were black Senegalese. Even though I was a little boy at the time, I remember being appalled at how the enlisted men were treated, and I can still recall walking past makeshift tents and seeing where soldiers being disciplined had been shackled outside, and chained like dogs. A French officer and his wife "displaced" my family from a room on the top floor of our house and we had to share kitchen and bathroom privileges with them. The house was "under occupation" until 1930, when all French troops left Germany. As young as I was, I had been kept quite sheltered during those years and I was largely unaffected by the unusual situation. I have no idea how my sister Lotte, a teenager by then, was affected by or reacted to the circumstances at the time. The French Captain and his wife were decent to my family, and quite often shared with us items that were hard to get, or at that time not available at all in Germany, including an occasional piece of chocolate for me. What is difficult to visualize is how my mother was able to keep the kitchen kosher as her religion required, and her meat and dairy dishes separated, with the French officer's wife doing her own cooking. On the surface, relations between the two women were always polite, and arrangements and scheduling probably worked simply because they had to, and accommodations and concessions must have been made by both of them. Mother, of course, was aware of the fact that the French were in total control of activities in the house, and she had to be careful with any suggestions or objections she might have made.

For Jews, life from 1933 on had become increasingly difficult with each passing day, but it was November 9, 1938, the "Night of Broken Glass," or "Crystalnight" that truly was a highpoint in the hell on earth that has come to be known as the Holocaust. To better understand what the Kaufmann family and others endured, it is necessary to look back to their life in the late 1920s and until the end of 1932, when I was still a little boy growing up in the midst of a loving family in rural Germany.

4.

Childhood Memories

FROM THE PERSPECTIVE of a young man born in the United States in the1990s, daily life in 1920s Germany would seem like a whole other world. There were no cell phones or IPads, no Internet or Facebook, no video gaming, no major league sports, and no television. The list of technological differences in everyday life alone is without end.

In the United States, prohibition, gangsters, and "flappers" in short skirts were the order of the day. Automobiles, movies, and radios represented the cutting edge of modern technology available to the general public. Life expectancy was 53 years for males and 54 for females. Average annual income per household was $1,300. By comparison, life in Germany was not nearly this good.

The impact of World War I had been felt worldwide. A staggering thirteen million soldiers had died, along with untold numbers of civilians in "the war to end all wars." While no country's economy was unaffected, in Germany desperate times grew worse as food and commonly used products became even scarcer than they had been during the war. The average adult German citizen was exhausted, frustrated, and demoralized. But, what would life have seemed like to a small boy, born in 1920 and growing up in a loving family in a rural German town? With food on the table every day, a comfortable home, and the love and security provided by an extended family and the surrounding community, what does a child know or care about politics? Indeed, Hitler's politics were insidious, his horrific plans covert, and the details carefully kept from the adult population.

My sister Lotte and I lived with our parents in one of the "nicer, newer homes" in Drove. My father Leo owned a successful business, was the cantor of our synagogue and, in the absence of a local rabbi, the respected lay leader of the congregation. Uncle Leopold had died in 1920 before I could get to know him, but my beloved Aunt (Tante Hannchen) lived right across the street from the family, next to the family's butcher shop. One of my earliest memories was that, when I was about four years old and I didn't like the meal my mother was cooking, I decided to "move out." I informed my parents that I was going to live with Tante Hannchen and marched across the street to her house! Of course, by nightfall I got scared, cried and had a change of heart when I said: "I am still so small and already have to live with other people," while looking forlornly at the house across the street, and forgetting that it had been my own decision to "move." When told by my amused parents that I could come home if I wanted to, I quickly ran across the street with a bundle of toys and sugar cookies in my hands. From then on I only went to 'visit' Aunt Hannchen.

Looking back, I still recall spending time with boys in the neighborhood, playing games, playing soccer and shooting marbles. This was home and town and open countryside, an ideal place for a boy to run and play and ride his bike. True for most small towns at that time, Drove was safe for children, and I could spend hours on my own without anyone ever worrying about where I happened to be. Even when an occasional caravan of "gypsies" came through town peddling their wares, it aroused curiosity, but there were never any threats to safety. Every little boy in Drove had a great deal of freedom.

Since I was little, I could not actually assist my father in the shop, so I began making deliveries for him that were within walking distance when I was around six years old, and later on a bicycle so oversized that I had to swing my leg through and in under the bar to pedal standing up. Having proven myself capable at deliveries, I was soon entrusted with more responsibility. At ten years old I was pedaling a new bike, fit for my size—out of Grandfather Gustav's store, of course—to customers even as far as two miles from home, delivering orders, and accepting payment for them. The butcher shop itself was unlike modern stores. There was no front showroom and no sales room, just a plain workshop. The big butcher block was in the middle of the room; knives and saws were in drawers, sides of meat hung on the walls and orders ready for delivery were stacked on shelves. A large walk-in cool room, sometimes supplied with huge blocks of ice twice a week, was connected to the shop, and all meat was kept refrigerated in it until it was cut into portions and sold. Almost all orders were delivered by family and part time help, while larger orders went by horse and buggy to hotels and restaurants in neighboring towns. Only rarely did a customer pick up an order at the shop.

My father bought and took delivery of the animals he butchered directly from local farmers or cattle dealers and kept them in the barn until he was ready to take them to be slaughtered in a big room at the far end of the property. The work in the slaughterhouse done, the meat ended up in the cooler until it was sold. Even though almost all of his customers were not Jewish, my father would not handle any pigs; he killed only animals whose meat would or could be kosher. Those were animals that had split hoofs and chewed their cud, mainly cows and calves, and an occasional sheep or goat that some customers might want to have killed for their own use. There was a small smoker area above the slaughterhouse that provided delicious smoked sausages and smoked beef, but only enough for family use. Making sausages for sale took too much work and time, and was simply not practical for the family operation.

As was expected of all children in those days, I had my own chores to do for the family. For our own use we Kaufmanns kept two cows, a flock of chickens, and Fritz, the horse, that all needed daily care. A large garden, where potatoes and asparagus, tomatoes, spinach, cauliflower and cabbage were seeded or planted, also needed regular tending. So did the strawberry plants, currant and gooseberry and raspberry bushes, A large meadow next to the house, pasture for the farm animals, had apple, pear, cherry, and plum trees whose fruit had to be picked in season, and there were eggs to gather, berries to pick, butter to churn, and pickles to brine. I was often kept busy digging or planting in the garden and helping with harvesting fruits and vegetables, while mother Else, aunt Hannchen and her hired live-in help, usually a young local farm girl, canned, pickled and prepared for storage whatever would be used later during the year, and would help especially during the winter months. When the girl, who during the week helped aunt Hannchen in the house and also milked the cows that were in the barn had her usual Sundays off, I, once I was old and strong enough often replaced a neighbor who on Sundays used to do the barn chores. I milked the cows, fed and watered them and the horse and mucked out the stable. I learned responsibility and acquired a strong work ethic, and rather than feeling overburdened by my chores I felt valued that I was part of my family's success.

At age six, I attended the three-room local public school, where grades from first through eighth were taught, and after which at about age 14 most children either went to vocational schools or worked in factories or on farms. Hours were from eight in the morning until noon, then a two hour break for lunch at home, and the walk back to school for classes from two until four, learning the three Rs. (Reading, wRiting and aRithmetic) On my way to school I passed a pond that in winter froze up and was always a temptation for many children to go ice skating. Not to lose out, I often ran home, gulped down my lunch, grabbed my skates and was on the pond until it was time to go back to school, and I also spent some time there after school, simply having parked my skates in somebody's yard near the pond. Once some friends and I lost track of time, were late to school and we were ordered to hold our hands out, palms up. The reed stick had its effect, and I never again came late to school after lunch and ice skating. The reaction of my parents, when I told them what had happened: "It served you right!"

In 1930, after the French occupants had left our home, my parents faced an important decision. Aunt Hannchen, who for several years had lived with just the maid in the big five-bedroom house—her brother-in-law Abraham, her husband Leopold's brother, had been living there until he died in 1928—now asked us to move in with her. Since the butcher shop and the outbuildings, laundry room, hay barn, wood shed, stable and abattoir were all near her house anyhow, and over time my mother had helped aunt Hannchen with many chores in her house already, the decision to move was made, much as my mother Else regretted it. She anticipated problems with kitchen "seniority," suspecting that aunt Hannchen would not step back and let her take over. Her fears were confirmed, and she ended up spending more time than she used to with her husband in the shop or with neighbors. She did however get her way when she made one demand before she was going to move: "Not until there is indoor plumbing!" Modern for its time when it had been built, the big house had electricity and running water, but indoor plumbing was not yet commonly available in the country at that time. Also, the proverbial outhouse was some distance away from the living quarters, past the butcher shop, the hay barn and the stable, and a necessary walk to it on cold winter nights must always have seemed exceptionally long.

Grandfather Gustav's men came, and a few days after they and some local craftsmen did their job to my mother's satisfaction, the move from house "Hauptstrasse number 32" to house number 57 across the street in Drove was made without difficulty, and the now empty house was rented out. Aunt Hannchen, by then in her seventies, did let my mother "help" her with cooking, and occasionally even let her do entire meals.

After four years of attending elementary school in Drove, I went to the Real Gymnasium in Dueren, six miles away, to get prepared for an academic career. The subjects covered during the six years I was there, all compulsory, included courses in German, history, geography, mathematics, sports, religion, music and foreign languages. For me it was six years of studying French, three of Latin, and one of English, and the hope of someday becoming a veterinarian. While school presented no problems, the six mile trip to it was not always easy. The first year, when I was ten years old, it was by a bus ride back and forth from Drove. The second year, because it was less expensive, it was by bicycle to the two miles distant railroad station at Kreuzau, and the train back and forth from there, with the bike stored at a customer's house near the station. And, at age twelve, it was by bicycle all the way, in rain or shine, ice or snow or freezing temperatures. The six miles often seemed endless, especially when the cobblestones and trolley tracks were wet, or when in winter even thick gloves did not keep my hands on the bike's handlebars warm. Academically, I had no difficulties, and I excelled at sports, but extracurricular activities did not exist. When I was about 13 years old, a new hobby got me into trouble: A neighbor had given me several pairs of carrier or homing pigeons. I prepared a pen in the loft above the barn for them, cut an opening into the roof and then I spent a lot of time watching the birds flying in and out and raising their young ones, much to the detriment of homework for school. A failing grade, of all things in music—I never, ever deserved better— resulted in an ultimatum from my father: "Gymnasium or pigeons!" The pigeons flew out of someone else's loft after that.

About a year before I started going to school, my sister Lotte, after four years of school in Drove had gone to the Lyceum in Dueren, also intent on an academic career—she wanted to study pharmacology. While at the Lyceum, she spent a lot of time in Buir, commuting by train from there to Dueren, because our parents felt she could be of help and comfort to our grandparents. She graduated (Abitur) at the head of her class in 1933, but by then it was already impossible to find a university willing to even accept her application. She found an office job in Cologne with a Jewish company, commuting by train from Buir during the week and spending weekends at home in Drove, until she married Fritz (Fred) Marcus in 1936 and moved to his home in Vettweis, a small town about three miles east of her parents' home in Drove. During that time, Drove itself was a quaint little town of about 800 people, most of whom were Catholic. In the 1920s nine Jrwish families were there—about thirty residents—but they were not the minority in town; that distinction went to the one and only Protestant family. The town had a post office and a blacksmith shop, a beer hall, two bakeries (one of which was Jewish), a cobbler, a Catholic Church, a Synagogue, a miller, a few grocery stores and four butchers (three of whom were Jewish). The citizens of Drove shared party-line telephones, worked locally, or traveled to Dueren to the sugar factory—a lot of sugar beets were grown in the area—or to Kreuzau to the Hoesch carpet factory, the area's major employers.

Life in the Kaufmann household was clearly defined, both by work and religious tradition. Although Reform Judaism had its roots in 19th century Germany, my family was more Neo-Orthodox than not. The traditions of *brit milah* (the covenant of circumcision), *kashrut* (Jewish dietary laws), *bar mitzvah* (the coming-of-age ceremony for thirteen-year-old males), and observing the Sabbath were faithfully followed. On the other hand, my father was clean-shaven and had no beard, a practice unknown to ultra-Orthodox Jews to this day, and my mother did not visit the local *mikveh* (bath of ritual immersion used primarily by adult females), a personal choice that led the visiting ultra-orthodox rabbi to decline invitations to any meals in our home.

Along with the foreign-language training I received at school, I sat with my father many a night as I approached my thirteenth birthday, learning Hebrew, reading *Torah* (Hebrew scripture), and reviewing the many blessings and prayers of the Sabbath service. My father prepared me for my Bar Mitzvah, the coming of age and being responsible for my actions from then on, a simple rite of passage that was celebrated simply with family and friends.

Preparation for the Sabbath started early on Fridays, with the women of the household cleaning and cooking, and father wrapping up the week's orders and other tasks. By sundown, the table would be set, the blessings said and the old antique oil lamp lit, while the live-in-maid tended to the chores that the observant family was prohibited from performing, and regular work would stop for a day of welcome rest.

On Saturday mornings, Jewish families, both from town and neighboring villages, would walk to the synagogue in Drove, where father, alternating with two other lay leaders, led services. Afterwards, an *Oneg Shabbat* (celebratory gathering after services that included blessings and food), would take place in the form of refreshments hosted at the Kaufmann's house for some relatives and guests before they headed home again. The rest of the day was spent with study, visits with friends and family, rest, and an occasional game of chess that my father had taught me to play. A brief prayer of *havdalah* (symbolic conclusion of the Sabbath), would mark the end of the day of rest and break with routine, and begin a new work week.

Standing out in my memory are the Jewish congregation's major celebrations of Rosh Hashanah (New Year) and Yom Kippur (Day of Atonement), Pesach (Passover) and my Bar Mitzvah, at which I did the reading of the entire weekly Torah portion. After my Bar Mitzvah, my father enjoyed when I was frequently asked by others, who had been given the honor to do the weekly reading to the congregation of the *Haftorah* (selection of readings from the books of the Prophets), to do the reading in their stead, in Hebrew, of course. I hated to do those readings and I only did them to please my father. For several months father also made me study for and do the reading of the much longer and more difficult appropriate weekly Torah portion. As prestigious an honor as this was considered to be, I do not recall relishing the nightly studies required, so that I could read flawlessly at Saturday morning services.

With the requirements of school and religion, chores and family life, it would be easy to imagine there was no time for simple fun. However, I was an avid and pretty good soccer player, and when in 1934 a Jewish sports club was started in Dueren, I was allowed to join, to be able to play soccer. It must be remembered that many activities for Jews were already restricted. Before I was even 13 years old, Jewish sports clubs and other Jewish cultural organizations came into being after Jews were excluded or expelled from community affairs where they used to be participants. The club in Dueren was fortunate to be able to use a local stadium until sometime in 1938. A Jewish Girls team, of which Lotte was a member, played handball there against other Jewish teams. Two men's soccer teams, one of juniors and one of seniors, took on opposing Jewish teams from other cities as well. I was one of two juniors who always played in two successive games, competing as members of the senior's team on the field after having just finished playing the regulation 90 minutes of the juniors' game.

The games turned out to be a lone opportunity to socialize with other young Jewish boys and girls, one of the few chances to meet young people from other cities, considering the confining conditions that already existed. Other than going for walks or getting together occasionally at the homes of Jewish boys and girls my age in Dueren, the games became pretty much the only entertainment possible. Restrictions were being felt more and more, and life had changed drastically after Hitler declared a boycott of all Jewish businesses on April 1, 1933.

5.

Before and after Kristallnacht

AS COMFORTABLE AND secure as I remember my childhood to have been, a historian would confirm that, at no time during this period would Germany itself have been considered stable, prosperous, or even enjoying "peace."

It was January 30, 1933. I was a little more than twelve years old, and within a few months of Hitler coming to power, the Kaufmann's world, and that of all German Jewry would never be the same again.

On April 1, 1933, a boycott of all Jewish businesses was enacted. Seven days later, Jews were banned from all government jobs. And so it went, bit by bit, the loss of one civil right following another, as Jews were reduced to less than nothing in terms of status, civil and human rights. Indeed, they were now being identified as official enemies of the State. We Kaufmanns were not treated like Germans anymore!

It took time at first—especially in the countryside—for some of the restrictions to be taken seriously, to be enacted, and enforced. In my part of Germany, Jews were now quietly and often with embarrassment, gradually excluded from public activities by their neighbors. Young and old were rarely invited any more to socialize with their non-Jewish friends. Thus, new forms of recreation—like the Jewish Sports Clubs, as well as Jewish cultural and social groups—began to appear, since Jews were by then excluded from all "typically German" activities.

In September of 1935, Hitlers new "Nuremberg Laws" were enacted. The first declared that marriages between Germans and Jews were prohibited, as were non-marital relationships between Germans and Jews, and the employment of "German" females under the age of 45 in Jewish households was also forbidden. With the enactment of this law, my family was no longer allowed to employ local girls in our home (although I remember that for a short time, until that also was prohibited, we had a young man, a neighbor, who was glad to come and take the girl's place).

Then, Jewish children were banned from attending schools of higher learning. As it had been earlier for Lotte, who had not been able to get accepted at a university any more, my education also suddenly came to an end. It did not matter that both of us were students with solid academic records and had the means and ambition for university and professional careers. We were simply told that at the end of the school year we would not be permitted to return to school.

When I was expelled from school in May of 1936 with little advance notice, my folks and I wondered: What next? It had become pretty apparent by then that emigration was more than just a subject of discussion around the dinner table among the family members. It had to be considered a possibility or even a probability. We also had to consider what would be a sensible way to prepare for leaving the country. The thought that the Nazi regime would implode was still a wish and a hope, but the brutal enactment and enforcement of new restrictions almost daily frightened everyone. Considering their age and lack of connections abroad, my parents felt that leaving the country for them would be just about impossible, and they were afraid of what the Nazis would expose them to next; their concern was for their childrens' future. They also thought that their home and what other resources they had would be enough to see them through, as bad as conditions were. As reasonable and sensible as my father always was, he suggested that a "manual" profession might be best for me, should I have an opportunity to leave Germany and end up in a country whose language I did not speak, because "If able to work with one's hands, one can usually get by."

Cousin Moritz Kaufmann (son of my aunt Paula) was an executive at M. Stern A.G., a huge salvage company in Essen in the Ruhr area, whose Jewish owners had their plant in Gelsenkirchen, some distance away. There, wrecking balls and torches made short shrift and heaps of pieces of various metals for reprocessing or smelting out of obsolete ships, railroad engines and cars, and other large pieces of equipment that were not fit for use any more. The plant had a machine shop, and my cousin arranged for an initial apprenticeship for me in the company's office in Essen, with the understanding that after a short time I would be transferred to the yard and its machine shop. After some weeks as a "gofer" in the office, I found myself at the plant, learning to work with mechanics' tools, acetylene welding, brazing and soldering, doing all kinds of equipment repairs, and also "learning" how to sweep the shop floor. Instead of being in the office in Essen at 8:00 in the morning, it now meant getting up at 4:00 AM, going by bike to the train station in Essen, loading the bike into the baggage car for the train ride to Gelsenkirchen, picking up the bike to ride to the plant and being at work by 6:00 AM. With only a short lunch break halfway through the 8 hour workday, I soon found myself on the cumbersome return trip back to Essen at 2:30 PM, arriving home by about 3:30 PM.

My parents had arranged for me to stay with aunts Selma and Henny in Altenessen, where they had a dry-goods store that they were forced to close not long after I got there. Since aunt Selma's three children, Kurt, Lottie and Marianne, all quite a bit older than I, had already left home, there was room for me, and I shared a bedroom with "Uncle Hermann," aunt Selma's brother-in-law, who a short time before had been let go after selling "Bamberg Seide," silks, for many years, and who was living in the apartment with my aunts. I had a hard time coping with good natured uncle Hermann's continuous loud snoring, and after several months of complaining that I had difficulty falling and staying asleep, and pleading with my parents, I was permitted to move. Dinner on weekends and doing little chores for them became the occasions for visits with the aunts from then on.

I moved to Essen and shared an apartment with a young man (Bachenheimer) who had been sent to Essen by Maccabi Hazair, a Zionist Youth organization. At the beautiful modern Jewish Youth Center "Bachus" taught Ivrit, modern Hebrew, and other subjects that could be helpful to anyone who might want to or was able to go to Palestine.

Since the Center was only a short walking distance from my apartment, and since emigration to Palestine was on my horizon at the time—there was nothing else—I joined a group of 16-17 year old boys and girls and took what classes Bachus taught. Since other public facilities were off limits to Jews by then, the Center had become the only place for social and cultural activities for young and old of Essen. Nice diversions were occasional bike rides into the countryside with friends I had made, or table tennis and whatever social events that were always going on at the Center. I also joined the Jewish sports club, "Hakoah Essen," became a member of the soccer team and played whenever a game could be arranged with another Jewish club.

My apprenticeship at the M. Stern A.G. began in June 1936 and was supposed to last for 2 ½ years, but by March 1938 the Jewish owners were forced to turn their company over to Mannesmann A.G., a huge steel firm. The company was immediately "aryanized" and all Jewish employees were let go. I went home.

Spending weekends at home with my parents in Drove, I went to Buir during the week, and from my grandfather's house I commuted by train to Cologne, where I was able to take a 4-week special Electric Welding course. After that I had a chance to spend about six weeks volunteering at the Jewish Hospital in Cologne, assisting the resident plumber in his routine. Having to make room for someone else, I was soon back in Buir again. By then my grandfather had managed to convince a Christian friend in Golzheim, a town a short bicycle ride from Buir, where nobody would know I was Jewish, to keep me busy in his automobile repair shop. Grandfather Gustav was always glad when any of his grandchildren were able to stay with him, especially since grandmother Caroline had died in 1933, after their 50th wedding anniversary party and my Bar Mitzvah. Since then he had been alone, with first a local Christian woman, and later a Jewish housekeeper doing the cooking and taking care of his home.

Then, while at work in the morning of November 10th, 1938, after the night that has become known as "Kristallnacht," the "Night of the Broken Glass," I got a frantic phone call from my sister Lotte.

6.

Lotte

SIX YEARS OLDER than I, Lotte was a "golden child" on many counts. A well-mannered girl, a dutiful daughter, and a serious student. Lotte was quietly respectful of the authority of her elders, her faith and her traditions. She had attended elementary school in Drove, and then went on to the Lyceum, a private school for girls in Dueren, where she was the top student of her class, and she easily made the Abitur (a scholastic designation used in Germany indicating achievement comparable not only to a high school diploma, but also an academic level equal today to the International Baccalaureate). Lotte had hoped to study pharmacology, but, like so many of her peers, that option was taken from her when Jews could not enroll in or were expelled from German schools and universities. The ironies leading up to Kristallnacht might have been laughable, had they not been so tragic. Just imagine how the following story involving Lotte exemplifies the insanity of the times:

Lotte was a beautiful girl, blond and fine featured. In 1935 she had some portrait shots taken by a professional photographer in Dueren. These photos of Lotte were so attractive that one showed up in the window display of the local theater with the caption "The looks of the typical German girl"(sic), at a time when Nazi rhetoric about pure blood, the Aryan people and "Real Germans" had become commonplace. Obviously, someone must have pointed out that Lotte was Jewish, because the photo disappeared almost overnight.

On another occasion, Lotte was having a conversation at the Markt Platz in Dueren with Mr. Winter, the "extremely Jewish-looking, but pure Aryan" (sic) sexton of the Catholic Church in Drove. She was yelled at by a passing Nazi, scolding how could she, a German girl, be talking to a Jew!

Thus it transpired that Lotte's academic life and career plans came to an end when she was nineteen years old. For a time she was able to find clerical work in an office in Cologne. One after another her friends began to shun her— actually crossing the street to avoid contact— as the venom of Nazism seeped into her community and her relationships with non-Jews, even long-standing ones, dwindled away. In 1936 Lotte married Fritz (later "Fred") Marcus whom she had met at a friend's house in Drove. Fritz had been studying weaving and textiles in Leipzig, but when his father passed away, he came home and took over his father's grain brokerage business. Lotte's new home was in Vettweiss, where she moved into the Marcus family house that she and Fritz then shared with Fanny, his mother. Their first child, a son, was born on November 10, 1937. By then, the Nazis were controlling nearly every aspect of Jewish life, including even what names Jewish children were permitted to have. Lotte's daughter Carolyn would relate the following story years later:

When my brother was born, he had to be named before my mother and he could leave the hospital. As required, my father went to the authorities to register his son's birth and to choose a name. By this time, Jews were prohibited from selecting any name that was considered "German." Instead, they were given a choice from two lists. One was of strictly Jewish names from Hebrew scripture such as Moses, Abraham, Jacob, etc. The other was a list of the names of the Catholic Popes! So my father's choice was between a name that would clearly mark his son's ethnicity in a country hostile to Jews, or the indignity of naming him for a pope. On that particular day, however, the registrar was an older, not very knowledgeable official and my father convinced him that "Georg" (George) was another form of "Gregory", which of course it was not. Thus, leaving the registrar thinking the boy had been named for Pope Gregory, my father came away with both a non-Christian and "good German" name for his son. When he returned to the hospital with the news, my mother wept.

7.

More Restrictions

EARLY IN 1938 another directive shook the entire Jewish population in Germany: A detailed list of all belongings, real and personal, had to be submitted to the authorities, itemizing each piece of property, each financial asset, and each piece of Jewelry — simply every item of even the smallest value. No reason for it was cited, nothing was confiscated, just submission of the list, but it was foreboding, an omen.

The second Nuremberg Law redefined German citizenship, and Jews were designated among those that were now to be identified as "Nationals" as opposed to "Reich Citizens," who were those individuals the Nazis determined to be of more "pure" German blood. Jews, who like war veteran Leo Kaufmann had proudly served Germany, were stripped of all rights of citizenship, torn from government jobs and discharged from the Military. They lost their right to vote and to fair representation — and in essence were denied even the simplest rights.

In Drove, these laws confused and embarrassed the town's population that Jewish families had been a part of as long as anyone then living could remember.

Nobel Laureate Heinrich Boell states in his article captioned *Die Juden von Drove* ("The Jews of Drove"), published in 1984 in the book *Koeln und das Rheinische Judentum* ("Cologne and Jewish presence in the Rhenish area") (as translated by me):

When in the year 1663 eighty- year olds remembered that at least sixty years before Jews had lived there 'for ages', one can assume that at the latest in the 16th century, if not earlier, Jews had lived there (sic).

Jews lived side-by-side with Christians in Drove, they looked and sounded like the next person, and had never been anything but friendly and accepting of one another. While everyone was aware of differences in religious practices and cultural celebrations, Drove's children played together, women shared news in the shops, men worked side-by-side, and everyone knew everyone else in town. Not unlike present-day America where Christians, Jews, Muslims and Hindus live together in the same housing development or apartment building, the citizens of Drove did likewise and thought nothing of the different routine of their neighbors.

Boell relates:

> To religious services at Drove came the Jews of Nideggen, Kreuzau and Untermaubach. They came on foot, and after services there was breakfast at Kaufmanns or at Leisers, and that was sometimes joined by non-Jerwish neighbors. Their life in the villages was taken for granted, as was their inter-action with non-Jewish townspeople. Bread was bought at Leiser's, the Sunday cake was also baked there; meat was bought at Schwarz-Treu's or at Kaufmann's or also, of course, at the non-Jewish butcher Nolden's, and paints and wallpaper were bought at Daniel's.

Boell describes how thorough the blending was:

> The Jews of Drove were not considered strangers, nothing about them was exotic, and since the townspeople had been enlightened about, and had been taken through the syna-gogue, neither was their religious service which, for propa-ganda purposes, often had been mystified. The Jews belonged. Their religion was different – but that had been known for

centuries. Considered 'strange' were the first Protestants who appeared in Drove around 1928. In Drove, the generosity of the Jews was legendary. There was always always something 'extra' at Schwarz-Treu, and when a woman had a baby, five pounds of meat arrived at the house so that the mother could gain strength and recover. Money was also loaned. The Jews were always good to the poor people, and no one knows how many debts have never neen repaid.

Families with opportunity and means to leave Germany had been doing so. Others, mostly young people, left with the help of sponsors in various countries, or of some still existing Jewish organizations that helped with finding a country that was willing to take them, and sometimes even assisting them financially. A few were able to flee illegally across the border into Holland, Belgium or Switzerland, and others found a home or haven in Shanghai, in China, or in some South American country where immigration laws were more lenient. Older and especially elderly people rarely had a chance to leave because they would be considered a liability everywhere unless they had relatives or friends living in some country who could both sponsor and support them. Still some who could not—or simply did not—believe what was happening around them would continue and could get even worse, hoped that reason and justice would eventually prevail. They decided to stay in the homes or communities in which they had grown up or in which they had lived most of their lives.

My folks continued to try to keep life as close to normal as possible. News came now and again of relatives who were making their way out of Germany, and my parents still hoped for the best, until November 1938, when our worst fears were realized.

In the weeks leading up to the autumn of 1938, more than 17,000 Polish Jews, most of whom had been living in Germany for decades, were rounded up and deported from the country. Zindel Grynszpan and his family were among the thousands literally driven from their homes. With nothing but the clothes on their backs, they were transported to the border with Poland where they were then dumped off—17,000 men, women and children—homeless and penniless. Zindel's teenage son was living in Paris at the time, and upon receiving news of his family's deportation, he went to the German embassy seeking news and help. In an altercation that took place while he was there, young Grynszpan shot a German consular official who died later that day, November 8, 1938.

With such speed that the plan had to have been in place long in advance, Hitler's propaganda minister, Goebbels, announced that this isolated action by a single teenager was "Proof that there was a conspiracy afoot against the German government, led by "International Jewry." In retaliation for this fabricated conspiracy, a nationwide attack on German Jews was set into motion on the very same day the official died. Beginning the night of November 9th, and continuing for the next 24 hours, gangs of marauding "Brownshirts" swarmed through the cities and countryside burning synagogues, breaking down doors of Jewish homes and businesses, smashing windows, breaking furniture and destroying whatever they could –- beating, terrorizing, and killing Jews in the process. This fateful event was to become known as "Kristallnacht," the "Night of the Broken Glass."

Lotte and Fritz were overtaken by the events of Kristallnacht as they were planning to celebrate their son's first birthday, on the 10th of November. Instead, Fritz was arrested and taken away, and Lotte and Fanny Marcus were ordered to vacate the rented house in which they lived. Along with one year old little Georg they managed to be taken to Drove by a non-Jewish friend and they then moved in with my parents and aunt Hannchen.

That was the day on which Lotte made that phone call to me while I was at work at our grandfather Gustav's Christian friend's auto repair shop, unaware of what had transpired during the night.

I got that call from my sister Lotte, telling me to get home to Drove as quickly as I could, and, saying in English, hoping that anyone listening in would not understand, that " All the synagogues are burning." I got on my bike and headed for home, past the vandalized homes of some Jewish families and our burned out synagogue. No sooner had I arrived at my home, which had not been touched by the roving mob, when our one and only local policeman appeared. He was a neighbor of ours, and his oldest son and I had been friends for years, usually biking to school together. He apologetically said that he had orders to arrest all Jewish males between the ages of 16 and 65 "for their own protection from the enraged German populace," because a young Jew had killed a German consular official in Paris. Johann Nolden, our policeman knew that my father was not yet 65 years old, and he said that he just did not "see" him, but that I would have to go along. I had never seen my father as angry as when he asked 'whatever for' he had spent four years in the trenches for Germany, and his wife's—my mother's—two brothers had given their lives fighting for the fatherland? Our good neighbor of course had no answer for him, and off I went with him, to the local firehouse, where a room had been converted into a jail.

There I met up with two other men who had also been arrested, and where I was to stay for two nights. Early the next morning, after our first night in jail, the policeman came and sent Isidor Leiser, the father of a young daughter, home to his family. Ernst Daniel, the other prisoner and I, having had food brought to us by our families, were picked up by a car the next morning and under Brownshirt guard we were taken to Dueren, where we were put on a bus with a number of other men who had been arrested in the county, my brother-in-law Fritz among them. From there we were taken to Aachen, the Gestapo, or Secret Police Headquarters. After a roll call and headcount, armed SA guards (Storm Troopers, i.e. Brownshirts) marched us to a train that took off for a destination unknown to us, making a number of stops to pick up more men along the way. Hours later we arrived at the railroad station at Weimar, near the Buchenwald Concentration Camp.

Chased off the train by SS ("Schutz Staffel," in black uniforms) men who used their rifle butts to hurry us along, we were taken to a line of waiting trucks that would take us to the camp. I was carrying an old red horse blanket that my parents had brought to keep me warm while I was in jail in Drove. While running from the train towards the trucks, I was hit on the head with a rifle butt by one of the SS guards who made sure I dropped the blanket when he yelled "Look, he's even bringing his red communist flag along."

8.

Buchenwald

BUCHENWALD WAS ONE of more than sixty main concentration camps operated by the Nazis before and during World War II; there were hundreds of smaller satellite camps in and around Germany. Buchenwald had the distinction of being the largest, and among the first camps to be built on German soil.

Constructed on a slope of the Ettersburg Mountain near Weimar, it was opened in July of 1937, allegedly for the purpose of consolidating the populations of several nearby prisons. Its real purpose became known within weeks after its opening, and it quickly gained the reputation of being the worst prison of its kind before the war. Technically, and despite the many thousands who died there due to its practice of "Vernichtung durch Arbeit" (physically working to death), Buchenwald was ironically not considered a "death camp."

Many of the larger concentration camps had a main gate that displayed a saying meant for those entering: "Arbeit Macht Frei," or "Work is liberating." At Buchenwald, it was "Jedem Das Seine" or, translated figuratively, "To each his own." In the eight years that Buchenwald was in operation, more than 238,000 people were incarcerated there, of whom at least 56,000 died at the hands of the Nazis. Tens of thousands more died while in transit to and from the camp.

Only in Poland were camps constructed in the first half of the 1940s solely for the purpose of the systematic termination of their inmates—the "death camps."

Buchenwald was renowned for starvation, illness, "medical" experimentation and torture. The camp's second commandant, Heinrich Koch was warped and sadistic and his wife was none other than Ilse Koch, known also as the "Bitch of Buchenwald," and the "Beast of Buchenwald," who gained infamy for having tattoos sliced from prisoner's skin in order to have book covers and lampshades made for her home.

It was to this hellhole that we were taken from our local police station, without warning or explanation. We had nothing with us but the clothes we were wearing. It was impossible to make sense of what was happening. It was true enough that tensions had been growing in the weeks preceding Kristallnacht, during which time one new prohibition after another was placed on the Jews of Drove and all of Germany. But then, following a nightmare of unprovoked violence in which Jews were beaten and killed, Jewish homes, businesses, and synagogues were destroyed, and Jewish property vandalized in acts of terror generated by the government, it was—unbelievably—the Jews who were dragged away and incarcerated. All of this was done officially "For their own protection from the enraged populace!"

I was eighteen years old at the time, and I had no idea of what was ahead of us when armed SS men brutally chased us off the train. Once at the camp, we were lined up, and after a roll call our heads were shaved. That done, the guards marched us to a barracks-like building that was open to the weather on one end. Layers of rough wooden shelves had been built, floor-to-ceiling, about three feet apart, and these were meant to be our "bunks." We were packed into this building like sardines. There was no heat, no blankets or no bedding, and it was cold in mid-November. With just the clothes on our backs to protect us from the weather, it was only by lying close together on the bunks that we even managed to keep from freezing.

We were all in shock—and could not have guessed what was in store for us. I recall that, while most of the German population knew about hard labor prisons for criminals, no one was aware of what really went on inside Concentration Camps. At this time no one could have predicted the role the camps would play in the Nazi's future plans for ethnic "cleansing." But these thoughts were far from a priority for me and the other Jewish prisoners. At that moment, our priority was simply to stay alive.

As I was getting my bearings along with my brother-in-law Fritz, and the thousands of others brought to Buchenwald following Kristallnacht, I also met up with two cousins who had been arrested in different parts of the country. Cousin Kurt Steinberg, who had done the genealogy study of the family, was picked up in Frankfurt, where he had unsuccessfully tried to hide. Cousin Eugen(e) Roer, the son of my aunt Julie, and his father-in–law came from Meiningen, in Thuringia. There, the goons had arrested men much older than 65 years, and one of them was Eugene's father-in-law, who simply could not survive the rough conditions; he became ill and died while many men stood by helplessly. All the Jewish men who had just been brought in were kept separated from the long term prisoners at the camp who all wore striped uniforms. The two groups were kept in separate compounds that were divided by tall wire fences. We, the newly arrived Jewish men, were not made to work. Largely ignored by our captors except for the occasional questioning of individuals, we spent the days milling around and watching events taking place on the other side of the fence, talking together, trying to stay warm, and trying to keep up each other's spirits.

As we looked on, it became clear that existence was horrific for the prisoners in the other half of the camp. They were a collection of gypsies, homosexuals, political dissidents, mentally disabled men, actual criminals, and Jews and others who had been imprisoned earlier. Those inmates were marched off early each morning under SS guard, for long hours of hard labor in the nearby quarry. From our side of the fence, we of the Kristallnacht action watched while those prisoners endured torturous treatment, hardly daring to speculate about our own fate. From our barracks we could see the others leave for work details in the morning and return in the evening. Then they were lined up for roll call and to watch "punishment" being meted out to some unfortunate souls. Some were hanged until dead; some were flogged until unconscious. Others had their hands tied behind their backs and were then hung up an a wall on what looked like meat hooks until their arms snapped out of joint and they fainted before they were cut down. The men were forced to watch a man stuck into a barrel that had metal spikes driven into it, and then it was rolled down a hill, where dogs finished him off. All this was done for the guards' own warped enjoyment. Only miserable, sadistic, beings could be capable of committing such atrocities. Man's inhumanity to man in action! And with each passing day, conditions grew worse in our compound: We were fed once a day. Lined up in columns, the men in the first row were handed mess kits and spoons by some of the uniformed prisoners from the "other side" of the fence who dispensed the food they had brought. A scoop of some unidentifiable slop was put in the bowls of the men at the front of the line, who ate quickly while standing in place. When finished, they handed the unwashed utensil and mess kit to the next man in the row behind them and stepped aside. This procedure continued until all 10,000 or more of us were fed.

There was no privacy whatsoever. There were no latrines. Simply slit trenches were dug in the open ground where we had to relieve ourselves. When the trenches were filled, long term prisoners from the other side of the fence that separated us were forced to empty the waste with buckets, carrying and dumping it elsewhere in the compound. What precious little clean water there was had to be preserved for drinking and cleaning the mess gear. There was very little water available for washing. We were consigned to living in filth.

Days passed without news from the outside world, and without knowing what was to become of us. Fritz and I, the two cousins, Ernst Daniel, the other man from Drove, and others we knew stuck closely together, trying to encourage each other not to become despondent. Through all of this, Fritz, Kurt and Eugene and I continued to stay relatively healthy. We were strong and fit, and determined to stay alive and survive the situation into which we had been put. What was not yet in existence at that time was the Nazi's plan for the "The Final Solution," that of the systematic elimination of the Jews of Germany and in all of Europe

By orchestrating and conducting the Kristallnacht operation, the Nazis probably calculated that by terrorizing, arresting, and incarcerating thousands of Jewish men, German Jews would hurry to flee the country.

The Gestapo let our families know that anyone who could prove that he would leave Germany before long could be released from the Concentration Camp. Not knowing anybody outside of Germany, either by mail or telegram, my parents contacted Hans Bloch, a young man who had become one of my friends in Essen, and who, in 1937 with his mother and sister had gone to the United States. He had been sponsored by his uncle Fritz Eichenberg, a renowned artist who had been in the United States for many years. They told him that I had been arrested, was in a Concentration Camp and could be released if it could be proved that I would leave Germany before long. They went on to say that I had a number on the waiting list of the German quota for immigration to the United States, but that I needed a sponsor who would send an "Affidavit of Support." (That was required by the United States Government, to guarantee that an immigrant would not become a public charge for five years, the time it usually takes for a legal immigrant to become naturalized and a citizen). "Was there anything he could do?"

Hans was rooming with his uncle's friends, Joseph and Ann Blumenthal, and he asked them how he could help his friend. They simply said "We'll do it," and with that they got the necessary papers together and informed The Kaufmanns that papers sponsoring me were on their way to the American Consulate at Stuttgart. With that information in hand, my father went to the Gestapo at Aachen and got them to authorize my release from Buchenwald. At the same time, one of Fritz's cousins who had been in the United States only a short time was able to collect financial statements from several people that, put together, were adequate to sponsor Fritz and his family. Fortunately, both he and I months earlier had put our names for a number on the German quota's waiting list of people who wanted to emigrate to the United States, at the time not knowing if they would ever be of use to us. The numbers on the list certainly did help us, and they made our early release from Buchenwald possible.

Thus it was, that in less than a month after having arrived at Buchenwald—and without knowing about efforts being made frantically on our behalf— Fritz and I heard our names called over the camp's loudspeakers, and then found ourselves back on the train from Weimar to Aachen, where we would report to Gestapo headquarters. After being made to pay for the train ride to and from Weimar, we were released. With guarded optimism we allowed ourselves to realize we were headed home to our families. On arrival in Drove, and in shock once again, we discovered that Lotte, George, and Fanny had all moved in with our parents and aunt Hannchen, having been forced to leave their house in Vettweiss. Fritz and I were weak, filthy and hungry, but we were home, safe for the moment and in the arms of our loved ones. We had been incarcerated at the infamous Buchenwald Concentration Camp and we had survived! Whatever the Nazi regimes' motives were, possibly because they were physically unable to handle so many men at the same time within the confines of the camp, some time after Fritz and I had returned home, most of the other men arrested during the Kristallnacht action were gradually released, even if they did not have prospects of emigration.

9.

Leaving Home

FRITZ AND I were home, having made it through the nightmare of Buchenwald. We also had the promise of a new home for ourselves in the United States, but the situation was tentative at best, and still very dangerous. It was now clear that there was no limit to the terror the Nazis were prepared to rain upon the Jews. Nor could anyone bear to mention the reality that not all of the Kaufmanns were making plans to leave Germany, at least not all at once or soon. It became increasingly difficult to imagine ever feeling safe or the same again. The family house our father had built had been Lotte and Fritz's wedding present from our parents. When, after their marriage, Lotte moved to Vettweiss, the newlyweds sold it to a family in town. With the proceeds they were now able to finance their upcoming passage and buy some of the household goods that at that time they were still permitted to take along, albeit only after paying a customs duty for even the oldest items that was equivalent to an "as new" price for everything.

The Government never ran out of surprises when it came to suppressing the Jews, and one of the hardest blows came early in 1939.

Early in 1938 all German Jews had already been ordered to make and submit that itemized list of all their possessions. Now, early in 1939 every Jewish person was ordered to pay 25 % of what he or she owned to the government to "Pay for the damages this Jew caused in Paris!" All jewelry, all precious metal, all items of value that had been on the lists Jews had to furnish, except plain wedding rings, had to be turned in. Some people had to sell their homes to satisfy the draconian demands. My parents had to sell all our parcels of land that had been used for animal pasture, not to a local farmer who offered a decent price, but to the local mayor, a good Nazi party member, at a ridiculously low price.

Lotte and her family and I were in the United States when later in 1939 came the next, most severe blow: the bank accounts of all Jews were blocked and they could only withdraw a certain small amount monthly for their subsistence. Anything else needed special permission that was rarely given.

Radios were confiscated, and that meant the end of listening to short wave radio broadcasts from abroad, the only source of unbiased news; listening was forbidden to Germans as well. And the telephones were disconnected in all Jewish homes.

It was December of 1938, and I, together with my parents, aunt Hannchen and Lotte's family of four were living in the large family home next to the butcher shop. The Blumenthal's sponsorship enabled me to emigrate, and the success of Fritz's cousin to put together an adequate affidavit that made it possible for him and his family to go to the United States had been a blessing. But, there was still the process of waiting for the affidavits to move smoothly through channels at the American Consulate in Stuttgart, and also waiting for our names and numbers on the German quota's list to be called. Lotte and her family got their visas in Stuttgart in February, and their passports shortly thereafter and within a few weeks left for Cuxhaven and sailed to the United States. I was to report to the American Consulate on April 20th, which incidentally was Hitler's birthday, and after passing both a mental and a physical examination I went home, visa in hand. My passage on the SS Washington for departure on May 5th was paid for before the Germans blocked all bank accounts and had been booked in anticipation of me getting my visa as soon as Hans wrote that the affidavit was on its way. I got my passport at the local mayor's office in short order, with the proviso that I leave the country within ten days. With my passport that was "adorned" with a big yellow "J" on the front page, I also acquired a middle name, " Israel," a middle name that every Jewish male from that time on had to add to every signature he executed or document he signed. All Jewish women were forced to take the middle name of "Sara."

There was little to do in the short time left, except to spend as much of it as possible with my parents and make farewell visits to friends and relatives. My hold luggage had been inspected and approved by a decent customs agent who did not assess a customs duty, and it was sent ahead to the Port at Cuxhaven. It had already been put together before I went to Stuttgart – a large steamer trunk that contained most of my clothes, some tools I had made, some small gifts for Hans and the Blumenthals, several German-English and English-German dictionaries, photographs, some professional books, and the disassembled antique brass oil lamp that had been in my family for generations. That lamp had been lit every Friday to invoke the Sabbath. Also packed was a prayer book that was an old family heirloom that my father had carried all through WW I.

Lotte, Fritz (now "Fred") , baby George and Fanny had arrived safely in New York, where HIAS (Hebrew Immigrant Aid Society) people met them at the pier and found a temporary apartment for them. They also found temporary work for Lotte as a domestic, and she was able to earn a few welcome dollars while they tried to find work for Fred. A job as weaver turned up for him at Frankfurt Woolen Mills in Philadelphia, and the Marcus family was moved to Philadelphia, where they roomed with another refugee family until they could find and move into an apartment of their own once their household goods arrived from Germany. Lotte managed to find work as a sewing machine operator, and she was soon able to write to the folks left behind in Germany that she and Fred both had "good" jobs and that they were doing well.

Then suddenly, it was my turn.

When May 5, 1939, arrived my mother was too distraught to accompany me to the train. With my father and a cousin who joined us to see me off at the railroad station in Cologne, I bade my loved ones goodbye, and believed that somehow, at some future time, we would be together again. I had my traveling documents, four American dollars, and a suitcase that contained what I needed for the voyage. The steamer trunk had been sent ahead earlier, to be loaded into the hold of the ship when it docked at the port at Cuxhaven and was readied for its return to the United States.

I recall the moment as though it was yesterday. My father was a strong man. But, at that moment he had tears in his eyes when we had to say good-bye. There was much that went unexpressed. His parting words to me were: "Don't do anything I'd have to be ashamed of."

Those words have guided me throughout my life, and I hope I would not have disappointed him.

And then, I was on board the ship, sailing for America. I could not have known it at that moment, but it was to be the last time I would ever see my parents again.

10.

Newfound Freedom

FROM COLOGNE, THE train carried me to the ocean port of Cuxhaven. The voyage, spent in tourist class on the SS Washington went by with great anticipation and without incident, and the ship arrived at Pier 81 in New York on May 13, 1939. Waiting to greet me there as I first set foot in my new country were Hans Bloch and Joe and Ann Blumenthal. Joe was able to speak a little German, I had one year of school English under my belt, and Hans (who would later change his name to John Blake) helped to translate. We four managed to communicate reasonably well as I expressed my gratitude for all their help.

The Blumenthal's apartment in Manhattan was only really comfortable enough for the two of them, and since Hans already was boarding with them, they had made arrangements for me to initially stay with friends of theirs.

Professor Helmut Lehmann-Haupt taught at Columbia University and his wife Lettie was a teacher at the prestigious Fieldstone School. They not only had room for me, but they were also delighted to have me stay with them for the rest of the school year, helping to take care of their two young sons while they were away from home. In exchange for room, board, and elementary English "lessons" from the youngsters, I lived in New York City during the first weeks of my new life. When the school term ended, both Helmut and Lettie were now free to spend time with the children themselves, and they arranged a summer position for me with their friends, the Esselstyns.

Dr. Esselstyn, a New York physician, had a gentleman's farm in Claverack near Hudson- on-Hudson where his family spent summers. To take care of the chores, the family employed a maid, a cook and a nanny for the three children; they agreed to have me spend the summer with them, filling in wherever additional help might be needed. So, for the next few months, I polished my English at the same time that I polished the Esselstyn's silver, washed their car, gardened, waited tables, washed dishes, or minded the children when the nanny was away. I simply did whatever needed to be done and what I was able to do. The summer passed quickly, and I soon found myself headed back to New York, with seventy-five dollars in my pocket and considerably more English in my vocabulary.

After a brief visit with the Blumenthals, who were destined to become my surrogate parents for decades to come, I was finally on my way to Philadelphia, to be reunited with my sister Lotte and her family.

11.

Starting over in Philadelphia – September 1939

WITH LOTTE AND her family waiting, and an apartment to call home, I arrived in Philadelphia to a joyful reunion with them. I had not seen them for more than six months, and catching up on what news and information was available from Drove since we had left was foremost on our minds. I then learned how Fred and Lotte had been able to make a living since they arrived in Philadelphia. They had both been able to take jobs while Fred's mother Fanny took care of little George, did the cooking and maintained the apartment. Fred was working as a weaver at Frankford Woolen Mills and had a part time job as night watchman. Lotte was a sewing machine operator in a shirt factory. I was anxious to get a job as quickly as possible, but above all I wanted to become an American citizen—wanted to get rid of anything that reminded me of my German background. Shortly after I had arrived in New York I made the initial move towards obtaining citizenship when I applied for and received my Green Card, the "Declaration of Intention," which I would need to become naturalized.

Meeting the Rovin family, the owners of the house on whose third floor walkup apartment where I now lived with my family, was the first thing Lotte arranged. Then came an introduction to the next door neighbors, getting familiar with streets and the surrounding neighborhood, finding out how I could travel should I find a job, and most pressing, getting used to a way of life completely new to me.

Fred and Lotte continued to help with my socialization. They took me to the "Central Club" which they had joined. Members met in a house in which mostly German Jewish refugees congregated on weekends for talks and entertainment, and where the English language was no communication problem since everyone spoke German rather than the still broken English many struggled with in their daily lives. The Club was the place where all "new" arrivals were bombarded with questions about conditions in Germany since they had left, because almost everyone had family members still there and was concerned and worried about them.

Lotte and I were constantly worried about our parents because once the Germans moved into Poland and began WW II on September 1, 1939, within just a few days, most of Europe was involved. This made getting out of Europe and not just Germany, much more difficult for those who still had the necessary documentation and the ability to leave. Before we left Drove, Lotte and I had managed to talk our parents into obtaining a number on the German quota's list for immigration to the United States, but we were now convinced that our parents would never leave behind our grandfather Gustav and aunt Hannchen who were both in their eighties and in excellent health.

About a week after I arrived in Philadelphia, someone mentioned to me that there was a garage owner who was looking for help. I found my way there, told the owner that I was a mechanic who had worked on cars in Europe and I was promptly hired. The hours were from 7 AM to 7 PM six days a week, Monday through Saturday and the pay would be eight dollars. The location was a parking garage where no vehicle repairs were made, and the main work routine was the washing of cars, keeping the floor clean, and pumping gasoline for customers. Another garage attendant would deliver cars to customers when they called for them—something I could not do since I did not have a driver's license. I always liked to see that this attendant was away delivering a car when a customer drove up to buy gasoline, because for pumping gas and washing a windshield, there was usually a tip of a nickel or a dime. When he was in the garage, the other man made sure that all tips were his own. With my weekly pay I could take care of the streetcar fare to the garage, help my sister with food and rent payments, and I even had a little money left for personal use or for saving. Saving money was much on my mind, because not long after I had left Germany, the Germans directed that anyone leaving the country could not pay their travel expenses with German money any more, which meant they would have to be paid for with foreign currency. The cost of getting our parents out of Germany would therefore have to be paid for with dollars Lotte and I would somehow have to come up with when—or if—our parents would be able to join us, and not with funds that they themselves might still have.

On a Sunday, several weeks after I had started my first job, Fred and Lotte took me to the home of Herbert Menko, the Central Club's soccer team manager who had started the "Jewish Athletic Club," the "JAC," and assembled the team. Herbert, his mother and two sisters had rented the house and the soccer team used the basement of the house as a "locker room" where the players changed into uniforms before they walked to the Nicetown Boys Club's soccer field for the games they played there. Herbert was glad to welcome me as a new member of the team and he introduced me to his family, one of whom was his younger sister, Mina. During home games, as well as those played away in New York or Baltimore, visits to the JAC's "Clubhouse," the Menko family home, was the usual routine, but I had another reason for going there: Mina. Meeting Mina was the beginning of a lasting relationship.

The garage job lasted for about two months, after which I found another one as a helper on a delivery truck that gave me the same weekly pay but was for only eight hours of daily work and a five day work week. A succession of jobs followed during the next year, including one of sorting dirty rags that I had to quit because the odor sickened me. Finally, I landed a job in a shop that built truck bodies and paid me 25 cents an hour.

Luckily for me, the Rovin's oldest son, Bill and I became friends almost immediately. Bill, an aspiring electrician, had quite a circle of friends and introduced me to a number of them. From then on, having dates was never a problem for me. Most dates were getting together in the parlor of someone's home, and because I was careful with my money, I only rarely took a girl to the movies. During one of the dates I met Morris Miller, a fellow who told me that he was working in a shop that was building bodies for commercial trucks and he suggested that I go to see his boss about the possibility of getting a mechanic's job there. Hoping for an opportunity of finally getting to do work I was trained for, I went to see Mr. Eskin in his shop and walked out having been hired with a starting pay of 25 cents an hour, and the promise of a raise as soon as I had proven myself. After quitting my previous job, I now started doing sheet metal work, welding and brazing and soldering; all work I was familiar with. And, after only a few weeks I got a 5 cent an hour pay raise. Several months later I felt I deserved another pay increase and asked for one. When Mr. Eskin told me that I would have to wait until times and conditions improved, I decided to look for a better paying job.

Ever since Lotte and I had left Germany, we kept up correspondence with our parents as regularly as possible, always careful not to mention anything the Nazis might find objectionable, since every letter going in either direction was censored. We knew that when our parents wrote that they were doing well, it was just to get their letter past the censors. Most mail from them was limited to information about the whereabouts and health of friends and family members. They did not dare to even hint at what they were exposed to. Not surprisingly, shortly after my departure grandfather Gustav moved from Buir and joined the Kaufmanns in our house in Drove. Even though we were just scraping by, both Lotte and I in our letters to the parents wrote that we had been lucky, exaggerating how well we were doing already, and that it would be absolutely no problem to take care of them when they arrived in America. We also suggested that after that it would be easy to get grandfather and aunt Hannchen to come here as well. That conditions for them had worsened became obvious to us when our father Leo wrote that he had been to the Jewish Hospital in Cologne and had a hernia taken care of. I knew that my father had been living with that hernia for years, and the thought of not passing a physical exam at the American Consulate at Stuttgart must have forced him to get the surgery that repaired it. The deterioration of their situation must have been so rapid that it made even him willing to consider leaving, probably thinking that grandfather Gustav and aunt

Hannchen could stay in an old age home until they too could come to America.

By that time I had become familiar with the general work routine and how employees were being handled individually, having seen several come and go in and out of the shop. I had heard that Kensington Wagon Works, a competitor, was also building truck bodies and I went to see the owner, Bill Durst. After I told him how much experience I had, Mr. Durst offered me a job, with pay starting at 40 cents an hour, a chance of periodic increases, and, if I wanted it, a lot of overtime. I jumped at the opportunity. I left Mr. Eskin's shop at the end of the week and started working at Kensington Wagon Works. As required, I had registered for the Draft for military service and was subject to call. Though not a citizen, I had become eligible for call up since I had received my Green Card, the Declaration of Intention to become a citizen. Kensington Wagon Works was building truck bodies for Bendix Aviation, a defense contractor, and since I now was doing essential work that was defense connected, Bill Durst soon suggested to me that I apply for an occupational deferment from the Draft. The deferment was granted and I felt that I finally had a "real" job. Pay increases came as promised, and with all the overtime work I could get, I was often going home with 30 - 35 dollars a week and able to save quite a lot of it. I was hoping that sometime soon I might have enough money saved to pay for our parents' passage when they were able to leave Germany. Lotte and Fred, by early 1941, had also changed jobs for better paying ones and they were able to be a bit more generous in their lifestyle, even though they were not enamored with what they were doing.

I discovered an old 1932 vintage Buick in a salvage yard and, in order to make my family a little more mobile, I bought it for twenty-five dollars. It was barely in running condition and it needed work on both the body and the engine, but it was soon good enough to take me through a driver's test and get me a driver's license. With my boss's permission I was able to keep it and to work on it in the shop, on my own time and on weekends. And, in a short time, I managed to make it roadworthy and even to look fairly decent. I gave the car to Fred who was able to use it for several years. Another very important chapter in my life unfolded at this time with the development of my relationship with Mina. Mina Menko, a bright and precocious young woman who had escaped from Germany herself less than a year before me, was to play a major role in my life for the next seventy years.

12.

Mina

MINA'S STORY WAS one to match mine in its own right, and it bears backing up on the timeline briefly to relate how her family's journey paralleled that of the Kaufmanns. The Menko's history began early in the 17th century, in Heidingsfeld, a suburb of Wuerzburg in Bavaria, an area rich in history and German culture. Mina was born on May 15, 1919. Her family had lived in Germany for at least five generations or more, having probably emigrated from Holland during the 1600s. At that time the family's surname was Menki.

The first official record of Mina's ancestors was found in a German synagogue archive that notes one Rabbi Menki, who died in the 1680s and was buried in the village of Rodelsee. In brief, the record next lists his son, Rabbi Menki Katz (1671-1764), who in his turn had a son R. Loeb Menki (1710-1770). This Menki's son was named Ensle Katz (1760-1834), who was to become the father of a Loeb Menki (1803-1867). By the time of the birth of *this* Loeb (who would become Mina's paternal grandfather), records show the family's surname had become Menko.

Loeb Menko and Rosa Maimann married and had six children; Hannchen, Simon, Fanny, Pauline, David, and Abraham (b.1859). David, Fanny, and Hannchen Menko never married, and lived together nearly all their lives in their ancestral homestead in Heidingsfeld. Their sister Pauline married a wealthy widower (Adolph Rosenau) and in the late 1800s, moved with him to America where they settled in

Philadelphia, Pennsylvania, and she took over the care of her husband's household and his seven children. Pauline had sought her mother's advice before taking on the responsibility of such a large family and Rosa had responded sagely to Pauline "If he had five daughters and two sons, I would advise against it. But, since he has five sons, and two daughters, I think you will be alright." Pauline and Adolph would add three more children to the number.

Rosenau family members were already very well established as the owners of Rosenau Brothers Clothiers—famous for its "Cinderella Dresses," the "Shirley Temple" and "Deanna Durbin" lines—which is remembered still today for its fine dresses for girls. Back home in Germany, Abraham Menko, who had started his own piece-goods store after graduating high school, was sufficiently successful that he was able to bring brothers David and Simon into the business. Although Simon would eventually marry and move away, Abraham and David remained in Wuerzburg, continuing to grow in wealth, reputation, and prominence as respected members of the business and social community.

The early 1900s found Abraham Menko approaching fifty, well established as a businessman, and not married. He was formally introduced to a young orthodox woman by the name of Emma Strauss (from the village of Eubigheim), while she was visiting an aunt in Heidingsfeld. They courted and then married on June 4, 1912.

Emma was a modest country girl. Abraham, twenty-six years Emma's senior, urbane and mature, took it for granted that he would move his young bride into his ancestral home. Mina reported years later that this might have been the one time her mother Emma asserted her will, refusing to share Abraham's house—and, more specifically, the kitchen—with his "spinster sisters." So, Abraham promptly secured a rental apartment right across the street from his family home, and Emma contentedly set up housekeeping. Their first child, Herbert, was born on October 6, 1914; Rosa followed exactly to the day two years later, on October 6, 1916, and Mina, the baby of the family, was born on May 15, 1919.

Jews living in Germany had, for several centuries, known great favor, great misery, and all conditions in between, based entirely on the prevailing whims of the German aristocracy. From about 1820 to 1920, however, the Menko family was among those lucky enough to enjoy a period of relative peace, prosperity, and acceptance, the result of which was that their family rose into the ranks of Heidingsfeld's social elite. Despite rising inflation and difficult economic times for many, the Menko family remained relatively secure. For them and their contemporaries, a sense of belonging, and defining themselves as "German"—as much as, if not more than as being orthodox Jews— was the norm.

Life for the Menko children was one of comfort and privilege. They lived in one of the fine historic homes in the city, beautifully furnished and tended by domestic servants. They were kept happily busy with the events of private schools and social gatherings. They went on vacations with family, and were doted upon by their numerous aunts and uncles, both those living just across the street and those in America who regularly shipped them designer clothing and other lavish gifts. Mina Menko's young adult life would almost certainly have included a university education, world travel, and a promising future, but for three pivotal events.

First, during the very same year that Mina was born, Adolf Hitler launched his unsavory political career. Second, when Mina was ten years old, her father Abraham died, and Uncle David took over the family business, and the guardianship of her family. While David was well up to the task, caring and capable, Emma and the children were never quite the same without Abraham as the head of the family. Finally, in 1933, when Mina was fourteen, Hitler was named Chancellor of Germany, which effectively sealed the fate of the country, of millions of Jews, and of young Mina.

Where the Kaufmann family's Jewish community was spared the outright violence of Nazi tyranny a bit longer, the handwriting on the wall was all too clear for the Menko family who were then living in Bavaria. Social activities with non-Jews became difficult, then stopped, and were then forbidden by law. Soon, Jewish homes and businesses were targeted for vandalism and destruction. On the morning of the second day of Rosh Hashanah 1935, Nazi "Brownshirts" stormed through the streets of Wuerzburg, arresting Mina's brother

Herbert and a number of other Jewish men for no reason other than to harass and frighten them. Although the men were released later in the day, it was clear the time had come to leave Germany. In an interview Mina gave over seventy years later, she related:

My family was exceptionally fortunate. From the minute that Hitler came into power, my 'American' relatives kept asking us," Why don't you come here to Philadelphia?" Family was waiting for us. Required "affidavits of support" sponsoring us were no problem for our relatives. Jobs were waiting for us. And we had the financial resources. It was far different for us than for many others.

So, while sponsors and money enough to leave were not an issue for the Menkos, there were aging relatives to consider, together with home, history, and heritage. Determined to make sure his brother's family was safe, however, Uncle David began making arrangements to get Emma and her children out of Germany as soon as possible. Rosa was the first to leave, sailing for Philadelphia and Aunt Pauline's home, in 1936. Herbert followed in 1937.

Having made the decision to stay behind in order to care for his invalid sister, Hannchen, Uncle David, with the help of 18-year-old Mina, set about securing passage for her, Emma, and whatever belongings the government would allow them to take. It was the autumn of 1938. In later years, Mina would recall:

My mother and I began to prepare to come to the United States. We were required to make extensive lists of everything we intended to take with us, down to the smallest item. Even the oldest handkerchief had to be listed, along with its value as if it were new, for the Nazi's review and 'approval.' As you can imagine, such an inventory was a tremendous amount of work, and my mother was helpless. As you might also imagine, I was always wondering what we might be able to sneak past the Nazis. I wanted very much to pack my father's gold coin collection, but my Uncle David said 'No, it's much too dangerous!' We fought about it and my uncle finally said, 'I do not approve, but I cannot keep you from taking your share.' Well, after that I took my share of gold coins and sewed them as best as I could into the old mattresses we were taking. It was not a simple matter because gold is so heavy. I would weigh the coins in my hand, and then sew them into a mattress in small, equally distributed amounts. Of course, with today's x-rays and other technology, I never would have gotten away with it…but, there were no such techniques back then. Still, I now realize what a risk I took!

The Menko's house was filled with generations of heirlooms and valuable collections, the majority of which could not be taken out of the country—indeed, they could only be sold for a tiny fraction of their real worth, to the Nazis. So, young Mina, with a uniformed customs agent watching every move, took charge of the packing. With him and her uncle she went to the nearby synagogue and out of the ark she took a Torah scroll that her father had commissioned to be written before he ever married her mother. It later turned out that it had been written by a scribe who was one of her mother's uncles. Determined to take that scroll with her to the United States, she had obtained permission from the authorities to take it out of the synagogue, but she was ordered to remove and leave all its decorative silver ornaments behind. The Torah was packed with other household goods after the three returned to the house, and when the agent once left the room for a few minutes, Mina covertly managed to switch and pack the family's good silver instead of the everyday flatware. She had buried a few small pieces of jewelry in a jar of cold cream, and after the packing was done and the moving van and the customs agent had left, she helped her uncle to cement the rest of her father's gold coins into a basement wall in the family home, hoping to be able to retrieve them one day. She and her mother left the empty apartment and were going to stay with the uncle and aunt until they were going to leave. All the necessary travel papers had been secured, the fees and taxes imposed by the government had been paid, and the loaded moving van was on its way to the mover's warehouse, ready to be dispatched and shipped to Philadelphia. It was November 9, 1938.

Sometime during that night, Kristallnacht, or The Night of Broken Glass occurred. Mina and her mother were jolted awake by the sounds of yelling in the street and breaking glass. What followed was a living nightmare. They watched from their front window as thugs came through the streets, kicking in the doors of Jewish homes and businesses. They watched as windows were smashed, including those of the synagogue, which was near their home, and from which, only hours before, Mina had removed the Torah. They heard that the wife of a retired Jewish teacher who lived next to the synagogue had been dragged from her home, forced to pour gasoline around the synagogue, and set it afire. Worried about them, Mina and her mother ran across the street to be with her uncle and aunt. And soon "Brownshirts" kicked in the front door and broke into the old Menko family home that in times past had been a national historical site, its rear wall being part of the old medieval city wall. They shattered every window, smashed chandeliers, and broke every piece of furniture they could lay hands on—stopping only when they got to the bed where Mina's invalid aunt lay with a broken hip, with Mina and her mother standing protectively at her side.

At that point, and with their bloodlust still not slaked, someone among the terrorists looked around the room and realized the Menko's home they were in was not the one from which he had seen a moving van leave earlier in the day. He ran across the street to the apartment that Mina, her mother and Herbert and Rosa had lived in since their father had rented it from their non-Jewish friends, the Becks, and found it empty. Sparked with new ardor, the thugs stormed off for the mover's warehouse to finish their task, to get at the crates that had been seen on the truck leaving the house. Miraculously—and what they didn't know—was that the mover had learned of the attack on the city's Jewish families, and at considerable risk to himself, had hidden the loaded truck in the nearby woods. When the thugs came and wanted the Menko family's crates, he told them that he had shipped them off already. With what could only be seen as incredible luck, Mina, her family, and the vanload of belongings had made it through the terror of "Kristallnacht." After several days the mover risked sending word to Mina, telling her that their belongings were safe and on their way. There were a few more days of excitedly waiting for the departure date to arrive, and then Emma and Mina were aboard ship and on their way to America. With family, friends, ancestral home and country behind them, mother and daughter would be greeted by the Statue of Liberty on Thanksgiving Day, November 24, 1938.

Herbert and Rosa were at the Pier in New York when Mina and her mother arrived and they were glad to be off the ship, because Emma had been seasick during the entire voyage. Happy to be reunited, all four of them had to spend the night in a hotel in New York instead of traveling to Philadelphia where Aunt Pauline was awaiting them. A knee high snowfall had stopped all traffic and it was not until the next day that they could join the aunt whom they had not seen since she had last visited them in Heidingsfeld nearly ten years earlier. Rosa was living with her, and she had an office job at "Nanette," a part of the Rosenau children's dress operation that manufactured what ages one to four or five year olds wore, and Herbert, who lived in a rented room nearby, worked in the shipping room of the company's main plant, where dresses for girls up to about age fourteen were manufactured. In time his job changed to that of a salesman, visiting stores in New England with the company's sample lines.

In anticipation of having the whole family together, Herbert and Rosa had rented an unfurnished house that they planned to have the family move into as soon as the crates of household goods that Mina had packed arrived from Germany, and they could set up housekeeping. The lift arrived and the four Menkos settled in. While Mother Menko kept house, she made the acquaintance of some other German Jewish ladies and she soon had a lively telephone friendship going that helped her fill her days. She never did learn to speak English. Herbert, who in his spare time was instrumental in starting and then managing the soccer team of the "Jewish Athletic Club," offered his house as Club House, and its basement for use as a Locker Room for the team. There was always some socializing at the house after the games, and soon a new arrival, a young soccer player, caught Mina's eye. A friendship began that later turned into a partnership for life.

13.

More Roadblocks

IF 1938 AND 1939 had been years of turmoil and life-changing experiences for me in Germany, 1940 and '41 once again found me settling into a stable life in America, working hard and saving every penny, improving my English, and, although there wasn't a great deal of time left for leisure activities, playing soccer, socializing with friends, and having many dates with and growing closer to Mina. In the midst of all these pursuits however, I had never lost sight of my main goal, which was to find a way of getting my mother and father safely out of Germany as quickly as possible.

I continued to keep in touch with Ann and Joe Blumenthal since my arrival in New York, calling them frequently to share the news of daily life and visiting them when I could. On those occasions, the conversation would inevitably turn to the increasingly dire situation in Germany, and my growing concern for my parents. Joe and Ann were willing listeners who sympathized with their young friend's dilemma. My attempts to get my parents out of Germany seemed simply insurmountable by any standard. In 1941 direct travel between Germany and the United States had become all but impossible. The Germans resented the help this country was giving to Great Britain, and diplomatic relations between the two countries were tense, to say the least.

Ideally, Lotte and I had hoped to have our parents come directly to the United States to join us. But the U.S.—as did most other countries at that time—had strict quotas limiting the number of people they would admit annually. The combined allowable total of Germans and Austrians the United States would accept in 1939 was only 27,370, an excruciatingly small number, given the thousands who were clamoring for a place on the waiting list for immigration to the US. And Leo and Else's number on the quota list was obtained much too late to give them any chance of being called soon.

We had learned that some German Jews were successfully finding sanctuary in Cuba. To get there, people could await their turn on the German quota list and then get to the United States. A security deposit of about 1,500 dollars per couple had to be deposited with the Cuban government, which would be returned when the couple left the island. A number of families had been able to get to Cuba that way. However, Cuba was rife with political corruption, with certain of its leaders willing and eager to relax immigration rules in exchange for lining their pockets with the deposited money of desperate refugees.

The catastrophic journey of the *St. Louis* in 1939 is, perhaps, the prime example of how fraught with danger emigration to Cuba could be. The transatlantic liner left Hamburg in May carrying 938 passengers bound for Havana. Nearly all of the passengers were German Jews who had paid dearly for their travel and entrance documents. Yet, at the very last minute—quite literally as the passengers were about to step off the boat onto the dock in Havana—the ship was turned away by an opposing government faction, and its human cargo denied sanctuary in Cuba. Despite such egregious internal corruption, growing resentment towards immigrants, and anti-Semitism festering just below the surface of its society, Cuba still seemed the best and most likely the only chance for our parents to escape from conditions that were growing more dire by the day.

Then, in June of 1941, we received sad news. Our grandfather had contracted pneumonia, and, at the age of 85, his loved ones with him in his home in Drove, Gustav Roer died. The family grieved. At the same time, we were all quietly grateful that Grandfather Gustav had not lived only to endure a worse fate. It also meant that there was now one less reason for our parents to remain in Germany. Moving aunt Hannchen to live with some other relatives or to an old age home until she too could be brought to America became a serious consideration.

Coincidentally, I found out that the procedure to obtain entry permits into Cuba meant that 1,500 dollars per couple had to be deposited, and that travel for two out of Germany by way of Lisbon would cost about 800 dollars. The deposit, that would have to be paid directly to the Cuban government, may as well have been fifteen million dollars for all the difference it made to Lotte and me. We had managed, somehow, to save about 800 dollars between us—no small feat for anyone struggling to make ends meet in the midst of the Great Depression in the United States, let alone two recent immigrants in their twenties. This would be sufficient to pay our folks' travel expenses from Germany to Havana. But, another fifteen hundred dollars was a sum too impossibly large to contemplate. I shared my frustrations and worry with Joe and Ann Blumenthal, and being the wonderful people they were, they simply asked me when I needed the money, and said that they would gladly lend it to me.

I was overwhelmed by my friends' generosity. But, unable to envision ever being able to repay such an amount should some unexpected problems arise, I politely declined their offer. It looked as though there was going to be a war, I argued, in which case I certainly intended to serve in some way, and what if I didn't return? Joe's response was simple. If that should happen, he told me, I wouldn't need to worry about repaying the money. "Other than that," Joe told me, "I expect this to be a matter between you and my bank. You can return the money and the interest owed on it when you get your parents over here; whenever you get it back from the Cuban government."

I realized this was probably the last chance I might get to rescue my parents, and I accepted the Blumenthal's loan. The funds were transferred out of Joe's bank and deposited in a bank in Cuba on behalf of the Kaufmanns. The money that Lotte and I had saved, that would get our parents from Germany to Portugal, and then onto a ship from Lisbon to Havana, was sent to a designated travel agency in New York. Thanks to Joe and Ann's offer of help, a viable plan was finally coming together for the Kaufmann family to be reunited.

14.

The Blumenthals

OVER THE COURSE of several decades the Blumenthals went from being complete strangers to filling a role nearly as important in my life as the family I had left behind in Germany. And while Joe and Ann were certainly not the only people who came to the rescue of many a refugee, their generosity and kindness did more than just save my life—they became an inseparable part of my family.

Joe's sympathy for young Germans who were seeking a new life in America was understandable. His own father had experienced what it was like to be a stranger in a strange land. While Ann had come to this country by way of India as an orphaned baby and was later raised in the Midwest, there is little known about her family and her background. After an 8th grade education she came to New York and entered nurse's training that she did not complete. She married and moved to Georgia, where an unhappy union soon ended in divorce. Back in New York during the depression that in the 1920s engulfed the whole country, she went to work for the J. Walter Thompson Advertising Agency where she was extremely productive and successful. That was the time during which she met, fell in love with, and married Joseph Blumenthal.

Joe's mother's family had emigrated from Germany just before the Civil War, and at the end of the 19th century his father made his way to this country from Germany and came to Pennsylvania, as a teenager who was alone. The senior Blumenthal worked his way up from peddling housewares as a door-to-door to store salesman, to store owner and then to become a successful and respected businessman in New York City. The American Dream worked for and realized. Another of his dreams was to come true when all three of his children were able to attend American colleges. Joseph Blumenthal entered Cornell University, left to join the United States Navy shortly before the end of the First World War and never was inducted. An appendectomy delayed his entry into the Service, and the war was over before he could volunteer again. He returned to New York and joined the family business. At the age of 26 however, Joe realized that he needed to follow his own dream and he began seeking work in the world of books, the love of which would remain a compelling passion throughout his life. In 1924 he got his first job in the book industry when he went to work as a salesman for a New York publishing house. With the experience he had gained, and his former supervisor George Hoffman as a business partner, Joe in 1926, launched a small printing house named "The Spiral Press." The firm did well, and its reputation soon provided work with the likes of Holt Publishing and Random House. They designed and printed a collection of the works of Poet Laureate Robert Frost. They also had a lot of lucrative contracts until around 1930 when business in general, and printing in particular slowed to a trickle. When a new printing house offered to buy the Spiral Press' equipment if George Hoffman and his experience came with it, Joe and George agreed— it was an offer too good to refuse. Joe had his mind set on doing something he'd been thinking about for a long time, and this decision became his opportunity.

While George Hoffman stayed in New York, Joe and Ann Blumenthal set sail for Germany. Joe studied with the unsurpassed craftsmen in Munich and Frankfurt, aiming to fulfill a dream, of creating his own type of design. After a year, the Blumenthals returned to the States, with Joe's dream realized when his own design, called the "Emerson Type," became a much admired reality in the artistic printing community. After dabbling in teaching and freelance design for several years, in 1935 Joe bought equipment, got his old staff together again and got the "Spiral Press" running once more. The company enjoyed some prosperous years, during which time Ann and Joe were able to sponsor and thereby save the lives of several young Jewish men from Germany. In his book "Typographic Years," published in 1982, Joe only in passing mentions:

> As the calamitous decade unfolded in Germany, I signed papers that enabled five Jewish boys to come to the United States. One had been a student in the graphic arts academy in Vienna; another who enlisted in the United States Army became an interrogation officer in the front lines and came out of the war a decorated young major. All fought for their newly adopted country, and all later carried their own weight as citizens.

In 1942, after America's entry into the Second World War, middle-aged Joe would close up shop again, this time to go to work as a dollar-a-year employee at the Army Map Service in Washington since he was too old for the armed branches of the military. Type and presses went into storage, and work was transferred to Marchands Press that served Joe's customers as long as the war lasted, and until the Spiral Press was able to begin printing again. Joe's modesty and talent for understatement are apparent in his words and his deeds. Signing papers to bring an individual to this country obligates the sponsor to support the immigrant until he becomes eligible for naturalization, to become a United States citizen, and that usually takes a period of five years. Sponsoring five young men whom they did not know was quite a risky task for Ann and Joe. Several times they had to ask his willing siblings to give them some supportive financial or employment statements that, added to their own, showed that their combined resources were adequate for a sponsorship. Fortunately, I was one of the lucky recipients.

15.

Shattered Hopes

WE RECEIVED WORD that on December 5, 1941 our parents had been issued entrance permits to Cuba. An end to our heart-wrenching worry was in sight, and I decided it was time for a serious discussion with Mina. We had become increasingly close over recent months. Since there hadn't been money enough for a glamorous courtship, we spent long hours together taking walks, going out for ice cream or coffee, socializing in the homes of friends, and many a night just talking about our old lives in Germany and our new dreams for life in America.

With my parents' freedom within reach, it seemed to me that I finally had a future to look forward to, a future of responsibility to both my family and my new country. Nobody knew at that time that the Germans some time in 1941 had secretly issued orders stopping all exit permits and emigration, effectively making the Cuban entry permits useless. Between work and family obligations, and finding some way to serve should the country go to war, Mina and I agreed—sadly—that it would be best to put our relationship on hold. We talked late into that last Saturday night together, and then parted company during the wee hours of Sunday morning, December 7, 1941.

Before I had even made it into my bed that night, I heard the devastating news and immediately called Mina to tell her I was coming back to her house. All our joy, and our hopes were dashed as the details of the attack on Pearl Harbor rolled in. The next day came the announcement. The United States was officially at War. By December 10th Cuba was also at war with Germany. The facts were now painfully clear. No more exit visas would ever be issued by the Germans; all entry permits for Germans to come to Cuba were cancelled. All chances of getting Else and Leo out of Germany were gone, the money deposited with so much anticipation in Cuba was to be returned, as it eventually was, and once again my world reeled.

16.

In the Army Now

EVENTS MOVED QUICKLY now, in the nation and in my life. As soon as the United States and Britain formally declared war on Japan on December 8, 1942, a similar declaration was fired back by Japan, Germany and Italy on December 11, 1942. I was determined to enter the military as soon as I could, not only to fight for my new country against the Nazi regime, but—if at all possible—to work my way back to Germany and my parents. Someone more familiar with the machinations of war, government officialdom, and military red tape probably wouldn't have even considered such an outcome possible, but I was 21 years old, dogged in my resolve, and I knew time was of the essence. I was motivated by an urgent personal mission shared by few others .When the Cuban arrangement fell apart and we went to war with Germany, I did not feel right about simply continuing to work. I went to City Hall in Philadelphia in order to enlist in the Army, passed the physical exam easily and was then given a number of forms to complete. One of the first questions asked was about my citizenship status.

This would be the first of a number of hurdles I would have to clear in order to reach my goal. The problem was simple enough; I was not a citizen of the United States. Thus, I could not enlist in its military. Now that war had been declared, the precious 800 dollars deposited for my parents' travel was yet to be returned, and I no longer had need of an occupational deferment or savings, for that matter.

My disappointment was great when I was told I could not enlist as a non-citizen, and when I asked what I could do to get into this war, I was told to go to my Draft Board, tell them to cancel my occupational deferment, and then ask them to "call me up." This is what I did—and, instead of being able to volunteer for service, I was simply drafted into the Army. I was given the customary thirty days to wind up my affairs, and ordered to report to Fort Meade, Maryland on February 8, 1942.

I went home, gave my employer notice, and worked for two more weeks while I wrapped up various personal obligations, said good-bye to friends, and saw to last minute chores. Of course I spent as much of this time as I could with Mina. New Year's Day 1942 found us sitting in the Menko family's kitchen, talking once again about the future until past 4 in the morning. I mentioned that I had always hoped to become a veterinarian, but that the dream and the education it would require had both been killed by the Nazis. Still, I mused with Mina, it might just be possible to work with animals in some other way. Perhaps I would return from the war, buy a poultry farm, and bring my parents over. It would be an ideal place where they could keep active and busy in their old age. And as we talked together about the future, Mina and I also came to realize how much our feelings for one another had grown. Many of our friends got married shortly before the men left to go into the service, but though we knew that we too wanted to get married, we decided to wait until I got back, whenever that might be. Part of the reason was that I still hoped to see my folks again, and the other was that I did not want Mina to be tied down, should I not come back.

Mina too had concerns about committing to marriage just then. At that time she, Rosa, and Herbert were all working and together shared in the financial support of their mother. But, if Herbert was called into service, Mina reasoned, that responsibility would fall entirely on her and Rosa. It was a time of strong emotions and difficult decisions for us, anxious as we were, but practical common sense prevailed. I spent most of my last night as a civilian making plans with Mina, and in the morning I bid good-bye to her and Lotte, and the rest of the family. Along with a number of other new recruits, wearing civilian clothes for the last time, and my last 20 dollars in my pocket, I climbed onto an Army bus headed to Fort Meade, Maryland, on February 8th, 1942

17.

Camp Wheeler, Georgia

DURING THE LATE1930s, in anticipation of the possibility of the United States entering World War II, Fort Meade was one site used for the buildup, training and indoctrination of troops for war. As soon as our group of inductees arrived, we were issued uniforms, for both fatigue and dress, olive drab colored underwear, shoes, leggings, towels, a mess kit and a duffel bag that would hold all of our "government issue." During the few days we were at Fort Meade, our time was taken up by attending training, lectures, marching, drills, doing callisthenic exercises and listening again to more lectures. During orientation, we were asked in which branch of the military we'd like to serve, and—thinking to put my mechanical training to good use—I promptly named the Armored Corps or the Army Air Corps. Considering the authority or time that clerks had under the Army's existing emergency situation, I could forget about my preferred choice of branch of service. I found myself immediately assigned to the Infantry and before I knew it, with my duffel bag and a train full of other inductees I was on my way to Camp Wheeler, near Macon, Georgia.

On arrival at Camp Wheeler we were lined up, and as our names were called we were assigned to barracks that each housed a platoon of four twelve man squads and had a Regular Army platoon sergeant in charge. This was to become my home and 'family' for the next twelve weeks. We were issued old WW I vintage Enfield rifles; the new Garand rifles were being issued to trained tactical units that were ready to go into combat, and supply had not yet caught up with need. There were not enough of them available for training units. Along with three other platoons we formed a Training Company, and train we did. For three months we did little more than close-order drill, marching, eating, calisthenics, marching, sleeping, rifle practice, marching, infantry tactics, marching, range firing, marching, guard duty, and--marching. After several weeks, and only if the entire platoon had passed inspection of barracks and equipment on Saturday mornings, would we get weekend passes that gave us a chance to go into Macon, where we usually went to the United Service Organization (USO). There we did not have to touch our grand monthly pay of 21 dollars that of course included "room and board" from Uncle Sam. The local community provided refreshments; there were dances, and a variety of entertainment. Many of us met local people who often invited us into their homes, where we enjoyed Southern hospitality and home-cooked meals, always a nice break from camp routine and "army chow." Well known entertainers also sometimes staged shows at the camp's theatre. On one of those occasions Al Jolson, of the then very popular "Vox Pop" radio program interviewed me. The show was broadcast nationally, and since I was able to alert them, Mina and my folks back in Philadelphia were able to hear it. He called me "Joe" to make sure that nothing I said about my life and experience up to that point would in any way harm my parents who were still in Germany, should anybody find out about my background and make that connection. The show was a treat for all of us, and I went back to the barracks with a beautiful gift: a portable radio.

The training program at Camp Wheeler had also included several intelligence, or IQ, tests, and near the end of the basic training cycle, men who had scored high were called to Camp Headquarters and urged to apply for acceptance at Officer Candidate School. I was among those called, but the door that was on the verge of being cracked open for me was shut just as promptly when it was discovered that I was not a U.S. citizen, and therefore I was not eligible to go to OCS. Back to the ranks I went, and then on to my first tactical unit assignment. I shipped out, and, after a short leave "en route" spent at home, I traveled to Framingham, Massachusetts, where the

24th Infantry Division, or "Yankee Division," was headquartered. I became a member of the Medical Detachment of the 181st Infantry Regiment that was stationed at an old Civilian Conservation Corps, or "CCC" camp in Westerly, Rhode Island.

So far, military service was not moving me any closer to my goal, and news from Germany became particularly ominous and scary.

18.

Distressing News

AS SOON AS war had been declared, all direct contact with my parents, via mail or otherwise, was summarily cut off. On January 20, 1942, Nazi leaders held the infamous Wannsee Conference to discuss the enactment of their "Final Solution of the Jewish Question." This innocuous label was nothing more than a euphemism for a plan meant to systematically and deliberately kill all Jews, worldwide. During March and May of 1942 Lotte received four telegrams, forwarded by the foreign department of the German Red Cross to the International Red Cross and on to the family in Philadelphia.

On March 5th our father had written from home in Drove that he and all the relatives were healthy. The tone of his short note was casual and hopeful and raised no suspicion.

Then, on March 23rd a telegram came from our aunt Emma, one of our father's sisters. Her address indicated that two of her sisters were with her, and she was at a "Collection Center" in Cologne. The telegram was brief, the message clear:

> Dear Folks: Leo and Else resettled. Will notify as
> soon as address known. Our health ok, hope same
> of you. Answer to Red Cross here. Note our address.
> Aunts Emma, Selma, Henny

On April 7, 1942, Lotte received a third telegram. She did not know it at the time, but it was to be the last communication we would have about our parents. Again, it came from our three aunts.

> Dear Folks: Leo Else address Council of Elders, Transport Aachen at Izbica on Wieprz, area Krasmystako, District Lublin Generalgouvernment. If possible send money and packages. Health good. Aunts Emma, Selma, Henny.

Izbica was a Polish village establiushed in the mid-1700s into which Christians drove their dispossessed Jewish neighbors. For two hundred years the population of Izbica continued to be largely Jewish, largely orthodox,, provincial, and impoverished. Then, during the 1940s, Izbica, with its railway stop became a transit point, a stopover for Jews being "deported" to death camps deeper inside Poland, although in Izbica, the deportees were still unaware of their true destination.

This last letter from the aunts was typical of those the Nazis forced Jews to write to relatives, or wrote themselves, using information they had stolen from the previous communications of their captives. They were made to ask for "money and packages" to be sent to them, virtually all of which was confiscated by the Nazis upon arrival. We would never know whether this third telegram was a bona fide request from our aunts, or contrived while under duress, or indeed, if they were even alive when it was received. Whatever the case, the April 7th telegram was to be the last communication that Lotte or I would get about our parents.

The fourth and last telegram from the aunts, who were still in Cologne early in May, simply stated that a letter to our parents at the Izbica address had not been answered. There were no more telegrams after that. Not long after that last telegram from the aunts arrived, we learned that they too were deported, first to Theresienstadt, and then from there they were shipped to one of the death camps in Poland where they were murdered.

19.

Welcome Change

AT THIS POINT, I was about six weeks into my assignment in Rhode Island when my Detachment Commander became aware of my fluency in German, and my ability to speak some French. He decided then and there that my skills would be of much better use in a tactical unit rather than in a medical one. He passed on what he had learned to Regimental Headquarters, where orders were issued and, once again, I was on the move. This time I was transferred to the Regimental Reconnaissance Platoon, whose job then was to patrol the coastline of Maine, watching for submarines that might be looking to put saboteurs ashore. The platoon was quartered in Damariscotta in the Fisk House, an old hotel that had been taken over by the Army, and where the billets were much nicer for sleeping than the cots in tents at Westerly, or anywhere else I had been until then.

The jeep patrol work was simple and sometimes, I have to admit, even "fun," but again it was not the assignment I wanted. Still, there were the occasional 48-hour passes, and with friends signing me 'out' hours after I had left, and signing me 'in' again hours before I was back, I was able to spend a full 48 hours at home in spite of the many hours of travel time between Maine and Philadelphia. Those were precious weekends that I spent at home with Mina and my family.

Then, finally, I got a lucky break. In March of 1942 Congress had amended a Nationality law, relaxing the requirements of eligibility for citizenship for those who had served honorably in the US military for six months or more. By September of 1942, having completed my six months of service, I "qualified." I promptly filed the necessary papers and on October 13, 1942, wearing the army uniform of my new homeland, I was in Boston, where I became a proud citizen of the United States.

With my plan back on track again, I immediately applied for admission to Officer Candidate School. My application was approved by Division Headquarters that forwarded it to the Infantry School at Fort Benning, and soon I was on orders to report there. A ten-day "delay en route," time before I was to report, was spent at home in Philadelphia which cost Mina a lot of sleep, and then I was on my way once more to Georgia, this time to Columbus. It was now January, 1943.

I arrived at the "Benning School for Boys" with the appellation of "Cadet," having automatically been awarded the rank of corporal, a status that more than doubled the pay I had been earning at the completion of basic training. The 21 dollars pay per month had been increased to 30 dollars just after my basic training was over, and a corporal's pay was double that. I admit the increased pay was very welcome, although there was little time to spend it since, once again, nearly every waking minute was spent in intense training—this time in organization and leadership, military tactics, recognition of enemy equipment, physical training, field exercises, and endless tests with little time off. Still, in little more than three months, the strenuous workload bore commendable results. There was one moment though when, shortly after arriving at Fort Benning, I came very close to being expelled from OCS. In the midst of a typical after-hours bull session, another Cadet made a disparaging remark about "all those flat-footed Jews evading the Draft," immediately reminding me of the Anti-Semitism I thought I had left behind in Germany. I was "mad as a hornet" and told him "You know, you can call me an SOB, but when you talk about 'the Jews' you insult everyone near and dear to me, and I want an apology for that remark." Somewhere along the way, apparently, a rumor had taken hold that the Jews were "yellow," and I was more than ready to set the record straight. Thankfully, however, when the argument was taken outside, several buddies pulled us apart, since fighting in the ranks would have certainly been grounds for expulsion. Fortunately, the rest of the officer training course took place without further incident.

Thus it was that on April 23, 1943, I marched onto the parade grounds with all the members of Officer's Candidate Class #226. No longer being a mere Cadet, Second Lieutenant Ernest Kaufman, 01318310, was handed a certificate that stated that he had success-fully completed the requirements of the OCS course. I had joined the ranks of new officers known as "Ninety Day Wonders" or "Shave Tails," sometimes also called "Gentlemen by Act of Congress." We were a bunch of eager young men, as yet unseasoned by the experi-ence of war.

I received orders to report to Fort McClellan, near Anniston, Alabama, following a well-deserved ten-day leave. Once again, Lotte and Fred would see very little of me while I was in Philadelphia and Mina would demonstrate that she could function at work without sleep. Ft. McClellan was not the last stateside assignment for me, but I was considerably closer to returning to Germany, and more deter-mined than ever to fight the Nazis, and to discover what had become of my parents.

At Ft. McClellan I was put in charge of training new recruits, teaching them the same skills I had learned at Camp Wheeler just a year earlier. Training recruits however was only a brief stint for me, because after a few weeks I was detailed to participate in the "School of Practical Application." SOPA was a six week long exercise that simulated combat conditions. Several hundred men formed a number of teams that conducted day and night maneuvers, sometimes jointly and sometimes opposing each other as if they were enemies, with umpires monitoring and critiquing all moves. Scouting was practiced, as were tactical problem solving and rifle marksmanship, as well as the use of various other weapons, including some captured German ones. There was also camouflage training, and terrain training that involved finding specific distant locations in a densely wooded area with only a compass as guide. And there were always a number of surprise targets in the form of men or weapons that popped up sud-denly and required quick thinking and decisions by the individuals or teams that encountered them. We bivouacked in the field and a field kitchen took care of us. The six weeks in the field, with weekend breaks spent on Post, gave us an idea of what warfare might be like without exposure to the real danger, that of live ammunition. On one of the first weekends on Post, I spent 25 dollars of my first 2nd Lieutenant's monthly pay of 125 dollars on a gift to Mina: a lifetime subscription to the the 'Readers Digest.' Without interruption Mina received delivery of the magazine each month for over 65 years.

With SOPA training successfully completed, I eagerly awaited new orders, but I was disappointed once again when I discovered that I was on orders to the West Coast for probable deployment to the Pacific. Once again I took matters into my own hands and went to Post Headquarters to argue that my fluency in German and a working knowledge of French would be wasted in the Pacific, while it would be useful in Europe. I managed to persuade the Personnel Officer to cancel the orders sending me to the West Coast, and new orders were issued. In early September 1943, with a delay in route spent in Philadelphia, I found myself transferred to the Military Intelligence Training Center at Camp Ritchie, in Maryland.

20.

Camp Ritchie

THE SCOPE OF World War II demanded intelligence efforts beyond any the U.S. military had known before, and the installation at Camp Ritchie, a former National Guard post, was just one of a number of facilities that had been transformed nearly overnight into a training center for weaponry expertise, photo interpretation, order of battle tactics, linguistics, prisoner of war interrogation techniques and general intelligence skills. Some came to Ritchie as fresh recruits who received their combat training later; I came out of Ritchie primed and ready to be deployed to the "European Theater of Operations." Along with thousands more like me we would come to be known as the "Ritchie Boys" in a film that described our activities during the war. Our particular group of soldiers was made up of mostly young German Jewish and other European refugees who had escaped the Nazis by immigrating to the United States. Like myself, many had sought to enter the military as soon as they could, and to fight back in whatever way they were able to. Obviously more adept in our command of the language and knowledge of German culture and mindset than any typical American soldier, we were singled out for special training in military intelligence and psychological warfare.

The Ritchie Boys main tasks included interrogating prisoners of war and defectors, offering an insight into the enemy's tactics and strategies, and demoralizing German troops with targeted disinformation. This was the crash course in which I was immersed for more than two months. Luckily, there were the mostly free weekends, and the Hagerstown train station was close to Camp. I could easily hop on a train from there to Philadelphia and be with Mina and my family as much as possible. For Thanksgiving 1943 Mina and I had made plans for her to visit me at Camp Ritchie, but those plans came to naught when I was put on alert.

I went to Philadelphia for one last five-day leave before I was to ship out in late November, bringing home whatever could not be taken into a combat zone. While I had not yet told Mina that I was shipping out, she knew what was ahead when she saw me carrying the portable radio when I got off the train at the North Philadelphia Station, where she had come to meet me.

After a few precious days with Mina, friends and family, I was on my way again, this time to New York and a transatlantic trip aboard the HMS Queen Elizabeth. The Queen Elizabeth was the largest passenger ship ever built when she was launched in 1938. While she was meant to be a luxury ocean liner, she began her '"career" in 1940 as a troopship; her deck was outfitted with anti-aircraft guns, and the Cunard Line colors painted over in battleship gray. She had been designed to carry about 2,300 passengers along with a crew of 1,000. However I was one of some 12,000 soldiers and crew that were squeezed onto her for a New York to Scotland crossing at the end of November 1943. Cabins originally built to accommodate one or two passengers were now rigged with hammocks for up to eight men who rotated sleeping in eight hour shifts throughout day and night. Traveling on the QE might not have offered the most comfortable accommodations, but at a speed of 26 knots she was able to outrun German submarines and could cross the Atlantic in six days without a protective convoy. We arrived in Scotland in good time and in good shape.

And at last, I found myself closer to the action for real.

21.

Towards D-Day and Beyond

IT WAS NOW that my intelligence training would begin to be put to use. I was assigned as Second in Command to an Interrogation of Prisoners of War Team that was to be assembled under First Lieutenant Robert Kennedy, who happened to be from Boston, but was not related to the well-known Joseph Kennedy family. My presence on the team turned out to be critical, since Kennedy's German had been acquired in college and was hardly adequate for the tasks ahead.

Shortly after arriving in Scotland and after a train ride to the Salisbury Plains in England, a number of Ritchie 'graduates' landed with me at a British Army camp at Warminster, near Swindon, and Evesham. There, we got to hone our interrogation skills on German prisoners of war who had been captured in Africa and were being held in a nearby PW stockade. Even though prisoners of war, some of them were arrogant and difficult to get to talk, but the training we had received at Camp Ritchie, and familiarity with their German mentality helped us to break the resistance of some of the most stubborn ones. Of course, after having been interrogated a number of times, some of the prisoners actually enjoyed acting at being difficult to handle, knowing they were being questioned simply to give experience to the questioners. Having been captured in Africa quite some time earlier, they had no more usable information anyhow. And they did know that by acting smartly after they had told us about their military experiences, they could always wangle some cigarettes during our extensive questioning that often ended up just being a casual conversation.

After a few weeks my unit, IPW Team No.39, had been formed. Four enlisted men were assigned to it, and the team was issued two jeeps with trailers for their gear; the intent was that the team would be split up and function as two independent units. Once assembled, the team was attached to Headquarters XIX Corps, for duty under the G-2, the Chief of Intelligence of the Corps ["G" denotes General Staff , G-1 for Personnel, G-2 for Intelligence, G-3 for Plans & Training, G-4 for Administration, G-5 for Military Government] , whose units were training and getting ready to go into combat. The Corps was made up of the 29th and 30th Infantry Divisions, the 2nd Armored Division, the 113th Mechanized Cavalry Group and other supporting technical units. Soon after our team was formed and the men, all Camp Ritchie graduates, had become familiar with one another, it was split up and both units gave demonstrations of interrogation practices and skits to various Corps units, teaching them enemy order of battle and tactics. Giving demonstrations and skits to units of the 113th Cavalry Group later turned out to become quite important for me.

Down time came in the form of weekend visits to civilian homes in the English countryside. Severe rationing of food that had begun in 1940 found the British people hungry for 'luxuries' such as tea, meat, milk, eggs and cheese. Under such dire circumstances it might have seemed strange that townspeople welcomed American soldiers into their homes, if it had not been for gifts of food and items otherwise difficult to obtain that the 'guests' were able to bring. For entertainment there were weekly dances in Evesham, where American GIs and British Soldiers were competing for the attention of local girls, some of whom were also wearing British Army uniforms.

Strict blackout regulations throughout Great Britain prohibited even the meager glow of bicycle headlamps, let alone the lights of trains or automobiles, making travel after dark next to impossible. Difficult as travel was in the spring of 1944, I was able to spend a five-day leave in Manchester with several cousins, children of my father's sister Bertha who, like I, had also been able to get out of Germany. Another cousin, a daughter of my aunt Thekla had also escaped from

Germany and with her husband lived in Stratford-on-Avon. On a weekend visit with them I did not get to see a performance at the Shakespeare Theatre, but I did get to see the Ann Hathaway Cottage.

Not long after returning from leave, I was ordered to a top-secret meeting at a castle near Cambridge, where several of us who were trained in aerial photo interpretation were put to work. Our movement was restricted, and we were confined to the castle grounds. We examined aerial photos of a certain area—we guessed, but were not told— of France, trying to identify and describe locations of fortifications and gun emplacements in the area, but above all to find out, if we could locate German troops in the area, and if so, whether they were armored or infantry units. Forbidden to talk about where I had been and what I had done, it was obvious to me that planning for landing Allied troops somewhere in France was progressing, and I was not surprised when six months after my arrival in England I finally got into combat in Normandy.

The XIX Corps' 29th Infantry Division was one of the units that landed on "Omaha Beach" on June 6th, 1944. They were part of an Allied invasion force of 160,000 men that landed on various beaches on a fifty-mile stretch of the Normandy Coast. Suffering heavy losses, but securing a beachhead, the 29th and various assault units landing on other beaches began the campaign to liberate Europe, and paved the way for other units to follow.

Striking camp at Warminster and moving at night in a large convoy of vehicles to a staging area at Southampton, IPW Team 39 crossed the English Channel on a Landing Craft and got to "Omaha Beach" near Isigny in France on D-Day plus five. I was ordered to proceed to the Headquarters of the 113th Mechanized Cavalry Group. Colonel Wm. S. Biddle, the commanding officer of the Group that consisted of the 113th and 115th Reconnaissance Battalions, had watched me conduct the mock interrogation skit and demonstration for his troops and was impressed enough to ask Colonel Washington Platt, the G-2 of the Corps, to attach my team specifically to his Group. Lt. Kennedy and the other half of the team was to stay at Corps Headquarters to take care of administrative details and to further process captured prisoners.

Functions of the 113th were either reconnoitering areas ahead of infantry units or protecting their flanks, and often one or the other Battalion was also ordered to support them with firepower. With their light tanks and armored personnel carriers they were able to move quickly in and out of encounters with the enemy and to capture prisoners. Whether at Group Command Post or at the front in action with a unit, S/Sgt. Parker and T/5 Ruelf, my enlisted team members, who were both fluent in German, and I were up to the task and often able to extract useful tactical information from newly captured prisoners.

On July 1st I was informed that I had been promoted to First Lieutenant. With the advancing Allied Forces the 113th encountered and fought German units at Goucherie, St. Lo, Villebaudon and Percy. From there we advanced to Domfront, Verneuil-Le-Neufbourg and St. Germain, and then past Beaumont-sur-Oise and Turnay into Belgium. From south of Liege both Battalions helped to liberate and ended up in Maastricht, being among the first American troops to cross into Holland and coming close to the German border. All during the advances IPW Team 39 often managed to get information from prisoners that helped the 113th to save time and equipment, and above all, sometimes even men. Some of the toughest prisoners to interrogate were members of some of the SS Divisions that the 113th or 115th Battalions had captured. They were the ones who had been indoctrinated by the Nazi ideologists and had been led to believe that they were members of the invincible "Master Race," and were arrogant even when captured. On occasion, it took putting into practice all the psychological tactics that I could muster to break some of them, or some actions that the proponents of the "Geneva Convention" on the treatment of prisoners of war would have considered severe, even though no physical contact was involved. If it could save American soldiers' lives, I applied whatever tactic was necessary to get information out of them. On one occasion, during the advance through France, the 113th was approaching a huge forest that was thought to be heavily defended by German troops.

We were near the huge Foret De Breteuil, and we were trying to determine the enemy's strength before advancing. I suggested to Col. Biddle and got his approval to try an experiment. Two light tanks, with me riding in my jeep sandwiched between them, slowly advanced toward the woods. Standing in the open vehicle with an improvised loudspeaker, I began an intimidation technique that would become known as "hog-calling." Speaking loudly in German to whoever might be within hearing distance in the woods, I stated brashly that Germany had lost the war already, that our American troops were advancing rapidly, and resistance would be useless; also, that we Americans treated prisoners fairly. As a further inducement I added that they could count on getting American cigarettes. I was not exactly comfortable, exposed in plain view while the men in the tanks at least had cover, but fortunately we were not shot at. The next morning we advanced through the Foret De Breteuil without a single casualty, and collected almost one hundred prisoners along the way.

22.

Paris

A BREAK IN the rigors of combat came when in October of 1944 I was ordered back to the U.S. Military Intelligence Service Headquarters, a sort of Replacement Depot in Le Vesinet, a suburb of Paris. I became the Officer in Charge of a Military Intelligence Interpreter Team, an MII Team that, as the American forces were approaching Germany, along with interrogation of prisoners of war, was given as its primary function that of dealing with civilians who were encountered as well as with civilian authorities. The personnel to make up my team was to come from the United States, and it took several weeks before they arrived. That meant several weeks of light duty or even no duty for me and officers from other units who had also been ordered back to MIS for the same reason. When I left the 113th, Col. Biddle told me that he expected me back as soon as possible, and he also asked Corps G-2, Col. Platt to make sure Lt. Kaufman, along with his new team, would be attached again to his Group.

What could be so bad about going to Paris that had recently been liberated? I slept in a bed instead of on the floor of some half-destroyed house. I even got to see and enjoy more of Paris than many others at MIS, because my brother-in-law Fred's cousin John Schwarz was General Eisenhower's valet and was quartered in the George V, the best hotel in town. John knew the town and I got pleasure— and advantage—out of watching him 'operate.' I had only a few administrative duties most days, and a lot of free time.

The stay in Paris lasted a little more than three weeks and, after having been wined, dined, done some sightseeing, taken in some shows and gone out on some dates with John I felt rested and ready to return to action with my new team. MII Team 420-G was formed, with me in charge and 2nd Lt. Edgar Holton my Second in Command. Four enlisted men, Tec 3 Robert Renaud, Cpl. Vincent Von Henke, Tec 5 Siegbert Lorch and Pfc James Skolnik, all Ritchie graduates, completed the Team. Orders issued on 23 October 1944 for it were: "Will proceed without delay by organic motor transportation, reporting upon arrival to AC of S, G-2, XIX Corps." Issued its "organic motor transportation," two jeeps and trailers, the team soon took off for Headquarters XIX Corps, that by the time the team got there had moved forward to Kornelimuenster, a town inside Germany's border. My team and I were welcomed back at Corps Headquarters, where I introduced Lt. Holton to Col. Platt, who told Ed Holton that he "would find enough for him and his men to do" once he got settled. He then told me to proceed without delay to the 113th, where we were expected by Col. Biddle and his staff.

Not only were my military associates glad with my return, but there were also folks back in Philadelphia who were glad for another reason, and that was to get mail from me again on a regular basis. It had stopped arriving for several weeks, except for a request to Lotte from me to telegraph me some of the money she was keeping for me. She and Mina, not knowing that I was in Paris, had been worried, since I used to write to Mina almost daily, and they let me know in no uncertain terms how they felt about my neglect: "You're having a good time in Paris while we're worried to death about you!"

23.

The Roer River Dams

ALTHOUGH THE 390 mile long defense system of German bunkers, tank traps and tunnels known as the Siegfried Line had been successfully breeched, progress towards the Rhine River had more or less come to a standstill after the U.S. 1st Division captured Aachen. Severe fighting for control of the Huertgen Forest area, not far from Aachen, went on for months, causing very heavy casualties on both sides. Aachen was also the Capital City of the District in which I had grown up, and where I had last "visited" Gestapo Headquarters on my return from the Buchenwald Concentration Camp about five years earlier. Near the Huertgen forest were two dams on the Roer River that allied air attacks had been unable to destroy or damage, and ground forces had not been able to capture them. What made me wonder was why the Germans with much haste in the 1930s, when I was still at home in Germany, built the second dam, called Schwammenauel. Thinking that there might be some military significance, in addition to its purported hydroelectric use, I decided to investigate, and I came back to Col. Platt with a load of documents.

I had grown up about ten miles from the Schwammenauel dam that the Germans hurriedly built before I left Germany in 1939. The huge construction puzzled many people, because it was just downstream from the Urft Talsperre, another large dam. Since Aachen was the capital of the district in which the dams were located, I drove into town with my men and looked for the District Water Administration building. I was able to locate the site that had been damaged severely, and in a pile of rubble I found a safe that we managed to blow open. In it I found a treasure trove of documents that caused Col. Platt to send me immediately to Army Headquarters to brief the Army Engineer about what I had found before I even had a chance to translate any of the documents. It took me a week to translate the many documents that were a German study of what would happen if the dams were blown. It estimated how many billions of gallons of water would cascade downriver, the rate of flow, how large an area would be inundated, how long the area would remain impassable, and much more information that proved to be so important that attack orders for 12th Army Group, involving many thousands of men of the First and Ninth American Armies, in conjunction with British units, were rescinded immediately, and the planned push to the Rhine planned for early November 1944 was put on hold. It was not until February 1945, after the Ardennes Offensive of the Germans, called "The Battle of the Bulge" was defeated, that the Germans blew both dams to cover their own retreat, when the US First and Ninth Armies and the British Divisions were able to advance towards the Rhine River.

Had the Germans been able to blow the Roer River dams during our originally planned advance, we could have suffered heavy losses in men and equipment. Finding that German study when I did prevented a possible disaster from happening.

When I found the German military study about the dams, I was not aware of how important it turned out to be for 12th Army Group's planning of the advance to the Rhine River. My team's "After Action Report" for the month of November 1944 that I submitted to the Corp's Intelligence Officer was simple enough. It read, in part:

> On several occasions buildings and government offices were searched in various localities, and a number of documents of immediate value were procured. Amongst papers found at the RURTALSPERREGESELLSCHAFT Aachen (Rur Dam Co. Inc.) were all the blueprints used for the construction of all the Rur River dams, and an estimate by the Germans of how dangerous breaching of the dams might

prove down-river. At the WASSERWIRTSCHAFTSAMT Aachen (Office of Water Administration) secret papers yielded exact calculations by the Germans on the effects demolition of all parts of the dams on the Rur might have on the entire sector of the US FIRST and US NINTH ARMIES, as well as on part of the BRITISH SECOND ARMY sector. The calculations were supplemented by maps (1:25,000) and documents, naming every village which could be flooded in the event of such destruction of the dams.

The irony of the tragic story of the Roer River dams is that, according to Howard Apter's article ("Epic Battle for the Roer River Dams," SAGA Book Special, October 1962), our troops were fighting so fiercely in the Huertgen Forest not because our Commanders were aware of the danger the dams presented to our advance, but to open up the area north of the dams for the drive to the Rhine. The Germans, however, resisted so fiercely because they thought we fought to gain control of the Rur dams. According to Rick Atkinson ("The Guns at Last Light," Henry Holt & Company LLC, 2013) there was a lot of discord among our senior commanding officers, and we suffered many thousands of casualties trying to get through the Huertgen Forest, as well as by eventually trying to get control of the Schwammenauel dam by attacking the village of Schmidt that is located on high ground near the dam and overlooks it. In his book, Rick describes at length the fighting for control of these two objectives as some of the most severe and most costly of World War II in Europe.

When I had gone into Aachen I had a toothache, and it got to be so bad overnight that I went to the dental officer at Corps Headquarters who tried to remove what turned out to be an infected, impacted wisdom tooth. After trying for more than two hours to take it out, the exasperated dentist, a Captain, gave up and said that he just did not have the proper "elevator" to remove the tooth; that he had to send me to the larger medical unit to the rear. After a two hour ambulance ride and a further two hour session in a dentist's chair, with the dentist's drill being propelled by an assistant working a treadle, the six hour ordeal was finally over. It was eight hours by the time I was back at Corps Headquarters. Luckily, Corps Headquarters was located in an undamaged heated huge office building, and I was glad to lie down on a cot, having come down with a temperature of close to 104 degrees. As sick as I felt, I immediately went about translating all the documents I had found and handed them to the Corps' Chief of Intelligence as quickly as I could, because my find in Aachen turned out to be of much more immediate tactical importance than I had initially realized. I recovered from the surgery and my temperature was back to normal at just about the time I had finished translating that huge volume of the German study.

The 113th was in a holding and defensive pattern since shortly after my return from Paris, and my team was detailed to spend most of its time at the Corps Headquarters War Room, where we kept situaton maps current and briefed visiting intelligence officers from allied units. The Battle of the Bulge was over, and when near the end of February 1945 most units of XIX Corps had crossed the Roer River, the river that most likely had given my mother's family its surname, I found out that the 126th Infantry Regiment of the 1st Division was taking an easterly tack and was heading right in the direction of Drove, the town where I was born. I asked Col. Platt if I could be attached to the 126th until it took and got past Drove, offering that I was familiar with the geography and topography of the area and might be of help, but that I primarily hoped to find out what had happened to my parents. My request was granted, and I joined the 126th.

We advanced into Drove against fairly light resistance and found that the Germans, because of the heavy fighting that had taken place in the area, especially in the Huertgen forest, had evacuated the entire population, and nobody was there whom I could question about my folks. My parental home had taken a direct artillery hit, but it was still in fairly good shape. Walking through it, I found nothing that reminded me of what had been my home. I was puzzled when I got to the attic where I saw what looked like a number of rough wooden partitions. Only after the war did I find out that all 26 Jews who had been living in Drove had in May of 1941 been ejected from their homes and were herded into my parental home. They were confined there until they were deported and murdered in March of 1942. The partitions in the attic were presumably to give some people a bit of privacy. The butcher shop and all other buildings were gone, totally destroyed. I left the house intending to go to the Jewish cemetery that lies on the outskirts of town, but I was unable to get there because the road to it was under heavy machine gun fire from retreating German troops. Drove was in our hands, and, as had been arranged, I left the 126th to rejoin my men, who by then, along with the 113th, had moved quite a bit farther into Germany. When I came back to my unit, I was greeted with "Hi Captain," and I learned that I had been promoted on March 1, 1945.

24.

Schiefbahn, March 1945

ALTHOUGH OFFICIALLY ASSIGNED to MIS Headquarters, attached to Headquarters of XIX Corps, and detached for duty with the 113th Mechanized Cavalry Group, my MII Team 420-G operated with a fair amount of autonomy, often "not under the radar screen" of my superiors. An example of this occurred when in the middle of March 1945 my men and I were in the vicinity of Schiefbahn. My grandparents and great-grandparents had lived in Schiefbahn and were buried in the Jewish cemetery there. I took a side trip and visited the cemetery which was in complete disarray. The tombstones had been knocked down, graves were desecrated and the grounds were in appalling condition. What followed is best described in a letter addressed to the Commanding General of XIX Corps by the Captain in command of Military Government Detachment I-10-E3, the officer assigned to Schiefbahn:

MILITARY GOVERNMENT
DETACHMENT I-10 E3

Korschenbroich, Germany

20 March 1945

Subject: Investigation of Alleged Assumption of Military Government Function.

To : Commanding General, XIX Corps, APO 270, U.S. Army
(Attn: A.C. of S., G-5)

1. In accordance with verbal instructions from A.C. of S.,
    G-5, XIX Corps the following report is submitted.

2. This report deals with an investigation of an alleged as-
    sumption of Military Government function. The incident
    occurred in an area under the control of the 2d Armored
    Division and clearance to investigate was obtained from
    the SMGO of the 2d Armored Division.

3. Summary of interview with Burgermeister of Schiefbahn.

    a. On or about Thursday, March 15, 1945 an American
        Army officer visited the Burgermeister's office. The
        officer identified himself as Captain Kaufman. The
        Burgermeister was directed to repair the damages to
        the graves in the Jewish cemetery of Schiefbahn and
        put the tombstones in correct alignment. The Captain
        indicated that he had relatives buried in this cemetery
        and was going to check at a later date to see if his in-
        structions were followed.

    b. The Burgermeister did not question the authority of
        the American captain and proceeded immediately to
        make the necessary arrangements for repair. He was
        uninformed as to the captain's status, i.e. either his
        branch, service, or military function.

    c. The day after the Burgermeister received his instruc-
        tions from Captain Kaufman, he, the Burgermeister,
        reported to the Military Government Detachment
        of Schiefbahn. He told the detachment MGO of the
        work being done at the cemetery and was given no
        instructions to the contrary. The Burgermeister did not
        report to the Military Government detachment of the
        visit of Captain Kaufman.

d. The Burgermeister stated that the tombstones had been displaced from their original positions years ago by the Nazis. He further stated that the workers at the cemetery reported to him that Captain Kaufman visited the cemetery on Saturday, March 17, 1945.

4. Summary of interview of Detachment MGO of Schiefbahn (Military Government Detachment I-3 E3). The Burgermeister reported to the Detachment that he had directed workers to make necessary repairs at the Jewish cemetery of Schiefbahn. Detachment MGO gave no orders to the contrary as he was not informed of Captain Kaufman's visit or instructions, and believed this cemetery work to be a routine function under the Burgermeister's supervision.

5. Captain Kaufman is not a Military Government officer, and Captain Bjerre, the officer having Military Government jurisdiction in this area did not give Captain Kaufman any authority to issue instructions concerning the repairs at the cemetery.

[signed:]   MICHAEL E. DIPIETRO
                          Capt.,Sig. C. MGO, Commanding

The letter made its way through channels to Col. Platt, who sent it to me, ordering me to answer "by endorsement." My reply:

To: AC of S, G-2, and XIX Corps

From: Ernest Kaufman, Capt. Inf. CO, MII Team 420-G

Re: Investigation of Alleged Assumption of Military Government Function.

1. The contents of the basic letter are substantially correct.

2.   No comment.

[signed:]   ERNEST KAUFMAN
                       Capt. Inf., CO. MII Team 420-G

The investigation ended there, when a smiling Col. Platt told me that he had received my reply. It was not the first or last time that I had taken action on my own that was not routine military procedure. The next one, barely two weeks later, was much more dramatic and had a lasting effect. My quick thinking and daring action may have saved hundreds, if not thousands of lives in the city of Einbeck.

25.

Einbeck

SPENDING THE LAST days of March mopping up operations that cleared the last remaining German troops out of the area west of the Rhine River, on March 30th the 113th also crossed the river. Slowed down only by blown bridges and sporadic resistance, it nevertheless moved rapidly through the Ruhr industrial area and Westphalia. With the German forces in full retreat before them, there was no longer a fixed "front line." MII Team 420-G was interrogating more civilians than captured soldiers. Many of the civilians were coming towards them, fleeing from the East, where the Russians were advancing into Germany, and gave the Team useful information about the area into which the 113th Cavalry Group had been ordered to move. Early in the morning of April 8th, after the 113th had reached the vicinity of the city of Einbeck, two men were brought to me for questioning.

Looking very scared, they told me that they had come from Einbeck, had been able to avoid detection by German soldiers, and that they had come to appeal for help. Their story was that normally Einbeck's population numbered somewhere around 12,000 people, but with the influx of refugees from the East in recent weeks the number had grown to almost 32,000. They said that there was a large Military Headquarters in town, and its Commanding General was determined to put up a fight to defend the city with obvious disregard for the possible huge loss of lives and property. Most people in Einbeck realized that the war was all but over and did not want the city and its citizens caught up in more bloodshed for what they by then knew was a lost cause. The two men sounded desperate, and asked if there was anything the Americans could do to save their city.

I listened carefully to what they were telling me, and then questioned them extensively about their own families, professions, activities, involvement in city administration, contacts with the Military—anything I could think of to make sure there was no "trickery" involved in their mission. They were able to convince me of their sincerity and honesty, and, after telling them that I would do what I could, I held them until near evening before I let them find their way back to Einbeck.

After the two men had left, and thinking that maybe, just maybe I could keep the 113th from having to fight a large military force when it was moving forward in the direction of Einbeck, I had an idea that later I always insisted had been simply a stupid impulse.

Early the next morning, my driver, who had volunteered to drive into Einbeck with me, tied a white rag to the vertical bar that was welded to the front bumper of my jeep. This was a bar that was designed to protect people who were riding in the jeep from wires or chains that might be strung across roads that, when tripped, could seriously injure people inside the jeep. We headed at top speed towards Einbeck, past several groups of German soldiers who seemed too surprised to try to stop us, until we were held up at gunpoint in the middle of the city.

I told the soldiers who stopped us that I had orders from my Commanding Officer to see the Commanding General and demanded to be taken to him. With two German soldiers sitting in the back seat of our jeep, we were directed to the general's headquarters. After my escort and I were out of the jeep and started walking towards the headquarters building, I turned to my driver and told him to "hightail" it back to our lines, not knowing what kind of reception I might be in for, and to 'tell them what I am up to'. I thought and hoped that with the white rag displayed on the jeep he might make it out of the city and back to our unit. Completely taken by surprise, the guards did not attempt to stop him.

Once there, I was led into a room in the building in which several officers were seated. When asked why I was there, I simply stated that I had orders from my Commanding Officer to speak to the Commanding General, and avoided answering any interrogatory questions, having been trained in and being familiar with just that kind of activity. I did have an anxious moment though, when asked where I had learned to speak German so well, and I was glad they seemed to believe me when I said that I had always liked language studies and had taken German in college. Obviously, not one of them had an idea that they were facing a Jew who a few years earlier had still lived in Germany and had now come back to fight them. Had they known—who knows what might have happened to me. Fortunately, they did not have time for more talk, because another officer came and escorted me into the general's office, where I came face to face with Lt. General Gehschnitt and his deputy.

After introducing myself, I stated that I had orders from my Commanding Officer to demand the immediate surrender of the city of Einbeck; that our American units were prepared to immediately attack the city in force, and that he, the Military Commander, would be responsible for any loss of life and damages to the city if he were to offer resistance, and that I, Captain Kaufman, was to wait for an answer.

The general listened to me without asking a question. He then told me to wait and had me taken back to the staff room I had been in before. It was empty now, all the officers were gone. Not feeling comfortable sitting alone there for some time, I suddenly heard the general screaming: "How could someone have let his driver get away." Well, that sounded to me like my driver had made it out of town. After what seemed like an eternity, General Gehschnitt appeared in the room, facing me and stated that, in order to save the population and the city from loss of life and destruction, he had decided to surrender with his troops and would accompany me to my Command.

The scene that followed was like something straight from Hollywood. The general and his deputy climbed into the back seat of their black Mercedes staff car while I, shaking like a leaf, sat in the front seat, giving directions to the driver. Behind the slow moving car marched some thirty German officers, followed closely by more than three hundred enlisted personnel. I slowly led the column of car and troops out of Einbeck and to the area that the 113th was occupying.

Once there, while an American Military Police unit that was attached to the 113th accepted and began processing the officers and enlisted troops, I took the two generals to the Cavalry Group's Command Post and a surprised Colonel Biddle. After making formal introductions, I ceremoniously asked the generals to turn their firearms over to Colonel Biddle, my Commanding Officer. When the generals protested hotly at having to surrender to someone of inferior rank, I politely told them that Colonel Biddle was in Command of American troops in this area, and, as such, he expected that the request to turn over their weapons be obeyed. Not having a choice, both generals placed their pistols on a table and were then led away to Corps Headquarters for further processing.

I was glad to see that my driver had made it safely back to our units and had reported what I was up to in Einbeck. Later, going back into Einbeck with troops of the 113th, and without any authority, I declared one of the two men who had come to ask for help, Heinrich Keim, to be the acting mayor of the city. Heinrich Keim was still mayor of Einbeck 20 years later, as I would come to find out.

26.

The War Ends

THERE ARE A variety of opinions as to the precise date that World War II ended, May 8,1945, the date of Germany's unconditional surrender to the Allied Forces, has long been celebrated; "VE Day", or Victory in Europe Day. Others say it was with a formal armistice in August, and still other historians claim it did not occur until Japan's surrender in September.

For many, however, World War II ended during April of 1945. For the remaining detainees in Bergen-Belsen and Buchenwald, the war ended on April 13th, when those concentration camps were liberated. For Benito Mussolini, it ended on April 28th, when he was executed by Italian partisans. On April 30th, it ended for the sociopathic mastermind of the war, when Adolf Hitler and his mistress Eva Braun committed suicide. April 12th, however, marked not only the day of President Franklin Delano Roosevelt's death—but also the day that World War II ended for me.

The 113th had moved into and occupied Wernigerode, a town whose history dates back to the twelfth century. Our troops met with little resistance as they moved into the city, and then bivouacked there the night of April 11, 1945. Early the next morning—along with Captain Hodnette, the Intelligence Officer for the 113th, and two MP's—I made my way across the open square to the picturesque town hall in order to meet with the mayor of Wernigerode. We were surprised by two SS soldiers who had made their way back into the city during the night. Suddenly, our group found itself taken into crossfire by the snipers. Captain Hodnette went down first, and then I was next, wounding one of the shooters as I fell. I dimly recall being dragged to the cover of a nearby doorway before losing consciousness.

My next memory was of awakening a week later in the 119th Evacuation Hospital with a Purple Heart medal pinned to my bed sheet, my torso bandaged, and my left arm immobilized and useless. As the 113th and the rest of my team, with Lt. Holton now having taken over, was continuing on to connect with Russian troops along the Elbe River, I was heading towards Paris in an ambulance. I was able to get word to John Schwarz who came to see me at Le Bourget Airport where I was waiting to be airlifted to a U.S. Army hospital near Exeter, in England. Later the same day, as I had asked him to, John cabled Lotte that he had "seen me on my way to England, and that I was okay."

Naturally, Lotte and Mina were delighted, thinking this message meant that I was whole, hearty, and on my way home. Days later, however, Lotte received the dreaded War Department telegram informing her that I had been seriously wounded and was in a hospital in England. The telegram read:

THE SECRETARY OF WAR DESIRES TO EXPRESS HIS DEEP REGRET THAT YOUR BROTHER CAPT KAUFMAN ERNEST WAS SERIOUSLY WOUNDED IN GERMANY 12 APRIL 45 PERIOD HOSPITAL SENDING YOU NEW ADDRESS AND FURTHER INFORMATION PERIOD UNLESS SUCH NEW ADDRESS HAS BEEN RECEIVED ADDRESS MAIL FOR HIM QUOTE RANK NAME SERIAL NUMBER HOSPITALIZED CENTRAL DIRECTORY APO 640 C/O POSTMASTER NEW YORK NEW YORK UNQUOTE = J A ULIO THE ADJUTANT GENERAL.

I had been shot in the back. Narrowly missing my heart and collapsing a lung, the bullet had gone in and out of my chest and ripped through my left arm, fracturing the bones and severing nerves, leaving me without the use of my arm and any feeling in my hand and fingers. With my chest wounds slowly mending, I was confined to my hospital bed for almost two months with my left arm in traction, a pin through the elbow and a weight pulling the shattered bones into proper shape. Although left-handed by nature, my school teachers in Germany had forced me to write with my right hand, and it wasn't long before I could write to Mina and Lotte myself, telling them of my condition. As they later told me, they were glad to know that I at least could "see and write." Care and treatment at the hospital was excellent, and the war in Europe ended while I was mending. A voyage home could not come early enough for me and for all the other patients as well.

I also corresponded with Colonels Biddle and Platt, who inquired about me during my hospital stay. From Col. Biddle I found out that Captain Hodnette was going to be all right and that the MPs had not been injured. With my left hand paralyzed, and my chest wounds nearly healed, I was put on a hospital ship bound for home in mid-July. Word reached me that I had been awarded the Bronze Star medal for "meritorious service." The citation read:

HEADQUARTERS XIX CORPS

Office of the Commanding General

20 July 1945

AWARD OF THE BRONZE STAR MEDAL
Citation

CAPTAIN (then FIRST LIEUTENANT) ERNEST KAUFMAN (Army Serial Number 01318310), Infantry, Military Intelligence Interpreter Team 420-G, United States Army, is awarded the Bronze Star Medal for meritorious service in France, Belgium, Holland and Germany, from 12 June 1944 to 27 March 1945, in connection with military operations against the enemy. As a member of IPW Team No. 39, XIX Corps, Captain Kaufman was uniformly successful in securing information from all classes of German prisoners. His interrogation of SS prisoners of war was particularly effective by reason of his novel and convincing appeal to their spirit of braggadocio. Captain Kaufman was later placed in charge of MII Team 420-G, XIX Corps. As CO of that team his direction of the activities of his men enabled them to secure much information of strategic importance to the Allied forces. In conjunction with the personnel of the XIX Corps Engineer Section Captain Kaufman secured the German Plans for the destruction of the Roer River dams and inundation of the river valley in the face of an Allied crossing. As a result of the discovery of the plans the Corps Commander and the Corps Engineer were provided with information that enabled them to plan and execute a crossing of the Roer River with a minimum of loss. The invaluable service and sincere devotion to duty displayed by Captain Kaufman reflect great credit upon himself and the Military Service. Entered Military Service from Pennsylvania.

(I might mention here that I did not discover the documents pertaining to the Roer River "in conjunction" with the personnel of the XIX Corps Engineer Section, as quoted in the citation. Only after I found and completed the translation of all documents in the German study did I forward them to the XIX Corps Engineer Section for inclusion in their planning).

The war in Europe was over, and I wanted nothing more than to get home to Mina and my family. Although I was able to walk off the hospital ship at Charleston, South Carolina without assistance, I had contracted viral pneumonia during the crossing and was consigned to yet another week in a hospital bed in Charleston. Transferred by train from there to Thomas M. England General Hospital in Atlantic City, I arrived in New Jersey on July 23, 1945. Mina and Lotte came the next day for our long-awaited, joyous reunion.

Emotions ran high. Clearly, the war was ending. Mina's brother, Herbert, who had been in the Army, had recently also returned to a new home that the three siblings together had bought before he entered the Service. And, while my injuries were serious and rehabilitation would be long and painful, I too was safely home. It did not take long for Mina and me to decide to celebrate my return by getting married as soon as we were able.

I was told that I was to have an operation on my left arm and that getting leave from the hospital was out of the question. However, I had negotiated myself out of tighter situations than this, and while Mina scurried to get a blood test and find a place to honeymoon during the year's busiest vacation season, I convinced my doctors that—having languished for three months without that surgery—another two weeks would hardly matter. Not surprisingly, I was granted my leave.

27.

Finally Married

THE END OF July 1945 found Atlantic City and the Catskill Mountain resorts a riot of high spirits—hotels were packed with happy couples and families celebrating the end of the war. There were no hotel rooms available at all, let alone any that observed Jewish dietary laws by serving kosher meals, a requirement that limited our choices.

Nonetheless, a plan was forged, and July 29th found us standing in Mina's living room before my former soccer teammate, Rabbi Max Forman, surrounded by our nearest and dearest: Mina's mother Emma, brother Herbert and sister Rosa, my sister Lotte, husband Fred, little George and Fred's mother Fanny, and, of course, our witnesses and honored guests, Joe and Ann Blumenthal.

The ceremony was simple and dignified, and above all brief, largely because it was beastly hot in Philadelphia in July, when air conditioning was still a luxury, and I was dressed in my only available uniform, my winter wools. I remember that I urged Max to make it legal, but fast—and he did. I had told him that, if he took too long to perform the ceremony, instead of crushing the glass as was the custom, I would kick him in his shin. Mina's mother later said that she was wondering if the marriage was valid, considering how fast Max performed it. Herbert, who was a pretty good amateur photographer, took lots of pictures. We all had an enjoyable dinner together, and then Mina and I, and Joe and Ann took a train to New York, where we were treated by the Blumenthals to a night at the Waldorf Astoria.

Morning found us on a bus to the Catskills, where Mina had managed to rent a room for a week, at a little hotel that served kosher meals. For the first time since we had met, we Kaufmans were really alone, and the next seven days found us sharing stories of the past, and talking into the wee hours of our dreams and plans for the future. The days and nights flew by all too fast, and before long it was time to head back.

Mina returned to Philadelphia and to her job, while I moved my few belongings from my sister's house to Mina's home before I headed for Atlantic City and the operation that would not happen for another six weeks. When it finally did, it marked the beginning of a long and successful recuperation. The war to end all wars had finally ended, and at the same time, Lotte and I had sadly come to the realization we might never see our parents again.

Years later, neither Mina nor I would remember the name of our honeymoon getaway in the Catskills, and Herbert, in the excitement of the day, would admit he had forgotten to put film in the camera. There were no photographs to mark the occasion. Nevertheless, we Kaufmans had crossed a threshold, survived the difficult final chapters of our youth, and now looked forward to a bright and promising future together.

28.

The Healing Process

MY RECOVERY PROGRESSED as quickly and completely as could reasonably be hoped for at the time. Muscles mended, bones knit, and slowly but surely, nerves repaired themselves in my arm and hand. With my left arm immobilized in a cast, I could do little more than mark time. I was not able to return to active duty, but I was far from incapacitated. So, once the stitches had been removed from my arm after end to end surgery on my radial nerve, I applied for—and got—numerous passes that allowed me to spend a great deal of time in Philadelphia. The only catch was how to best get home and back to the hospital as frequently as my passes allowed.

Cars were in short supply just after the war, but I had purchased and rebuilt a Buick several years before that served the family well until it was not dependable transportation any more. Even though I was at first unable to drive because of the body cast I was wearing until the surgery on my arm had healed, I bought a 1934 Model Ford that both Fred and I were able to put to good use. Fred chauffeured me from the hospital to Philadelphia, and back to Atlantic City again, and then had the car's use for the rest of the week until I was able to drive again. During this time Mina and I talked at great length about our future together. Would I be willing or even be able to continue my military career? If not, what would I do for work? Our talks returned to discussions from years before of the possibility of owning a poultry farm.

Never one to rest long or easily on "my laurels," I decided to put the time while waiting for my cast to be removed to good use. I contacted Rutgers University and discovered they had a three-month course in Poultry Husbandry, and then managed to orchestrate two consecutive six-week convalescent leaves. Traveling by train from Philadelphia to New Brunswick, I enrolled in the Agricultural School's Poultry Short Course, which I then easily completed.

When I reported back to England General Hospital, my surgeon was well pleased with my healing. But he also told me it could take as long as five years for me to recover to the maximum extent possible; that my left ulnar nerve was permanently damaged and would restrict the range of motion of that arm, and that further physical therapy and rest were a must. After a short stay at the Traymore Hotel in Atlantic City, that had been turned into a convalescent center for the military hospital's patients, I began a trek through various convalescent homes in the tri-state area that ranged from Atlantic City to Camp Upton, near Patchogue, Long Island, and finally to the Valley Forge Convalescent Center in Pennsylvania. The last move was intended to bring patients as close as possible to their homes and families. Between spending time with me at home, and visiting me while I was away, Mina—between my visits home—had a difficult time. She had her job, her chores around the house, and she was the one in the family who was doing all the shopping to help Mother Menko.

A fond memory was an exercise in physical therapy that I created for myself. As soon as the cast was removed, though with some difficulty, I was able to drive again. I felt I wanted to have more use of a car and by trading the Ford and adding $450 I was able to buy a 1938 Dodge Coupe that was mechanically sound, but it had a body that was a wreck as a result of an accident. The body and fender work was great therapy for helping me to regain strength and feeling in my injured arm and hand, but there was only one place available for me to do the work, and that was right in the street in front of the Menko's house.

Mother Menko was aghast! There was the awful looking car, parked right in front of her house. Naturally, there was much hammering, banging out of fenders, and painting going on all the time. At one point, the car was a combination of its original blue color speck-led with black, grey and orange spots of primer paint. The multicolor phase of its reconditioning lasted for quite some time and was the subject of comments, not all favorable, especially by neighbors, and also by family and friends. But when the final blue finish coat had dried, I had a car that was mechanically sound and looked very nice.

Another fond memory and highlight of this time, however, were the many drives Mina and I took through the farmlands of New Jersey when I was home, getting a feel for the availability and cost of poultry farms; imagining and planning our future together.

A highlight—and a much more precious addition to the family's life around this time—was the arrival of Lotte's second child, Carolyn, in July of 1946. Despite the pain of coming to grips with the loss of our parents, Lotte and I felt ever more at home in what had become our new home country, and we enjoyed our growing families.

29.

Back to Germany

IN 1946, THE War Department issued an order that promoted all military personnel who had been combat wounded and were hospitalized for at least 18 months. I was promoted to the rank of Major, and Mina and I especially welcomed the pay raise the promotion merited. It took until August of 1946 for me to finally regain some feeling and movement in my left wrist, hand and fingertips. Considering the benefits the promotion gave me, and the physical condition I was in, I wrestled with some thoughts about what I might be able to do in the near future, should I be discharged from the Service.

It was apparent that my surgeon's prognosis had been correct, and that it could easily take another three years for me to regain optimum use of my left arm, hand and fingers. If this was the case, certain kinds of employment had to be ruled out. Most of the German-speaking linguists who had served during the war had by now been separated from the military, and it might be worth trying to find out if some American unit in Germany could use someone with my qualifications and experience.

After discussing my idea with Mina, we both agreed that I would make inquiries about a possible assignment in Germany. I wrote a letter to Col. Philps, the Commanding Officer of the European Command Intelligence Center located in Oberursel, near Frankfurt, asking if there might be a place in his organization for someone with my background and experience. A quick reply came from Lt. Col.

Webster, the unit's Executive Officer, telling me that a request for me had been submitted to the War Department. Orders were soon cut and by November of 1946 I was on a Liberty Ship out of New York, heading back to Germany.

We had been told that Mina would be able to follow me "concurrently" or, in other words, almost immediately. To that end, Mina quit her job of being in charge of the IBM department at Rosenau Brothers that she had been promoted to when the war began, and promptly made all preparations to follow me. Upon my arrival in Germany, however, it became clear there was a "temporary" shortage of housing for Field Grade officers, and I found myself quartered at a nearby country estate, the Luisenhof, along with three other American officers, two of whom were also awaiting the arrival of their wives. The housing situation had developed because I was still a captain when I inquired about a tour of duty with the European Command Intelligence Center, and only quarters for Company Grade officers had been available for immediate occupancy at that time.

Life at the Luisenhof was thoroughly enjoyable, with Frau Gruschwitz, our hostess, and a cook and a maid taking care of our every whim. Food supplies for us came from Camp King, as ECIC was called, and meals were prepared by Klara, our excellent cook. After I had arrived in Germany I called Colonel Biddle, who by then was the Commanding Officer of the 6th Constabulary Brigade and had his Headquarters in Regensburg. When he heard that I was back in Germany, he immediately asked if I could join his outfit, and told me that he would love to have me back with his Command. Unfortunately, my orders were to report to the CO of ECIC. Had I been able to transfer to Regensburg, quarters would have been available immediately, and Mina would not have had any wait before she could join me. In the meantime, of course, frustrated Mina languished at home in Philadelphia, expecting the port call promised any day, but which did not happen until nearly six months later in May of 1947. When she finally arrived in Germany via the hospital ship Stafford, she found a fully furnished home waiting for her in Hoechst, a suburb of Frankfurt, as well as a second, even more delightful surprise. Since she was never allowed to have a pet while growing up, I had bought her a pedigreed German shepherd puppy named "Astor von Fahrbach" whom we promptly called "Peter," who immediately took over the Kaufman household and was instantly enamored of both Mina and me. For the first time since we had been married, Mina and I, and now Peter, too, were setting up housekeeping. Our transportation was now provided by the Dodge coupe that had been driven to Ft. Hamilton, New York by Max Rapp, who had become a friend of mine while I was in Essen, and who had also settled in Philadelphia. The car was prepared for shipment to Germany, and I was glad to take a train ride to the port at Bremerhaven to pick it up when I was notified that it had arrived.

I was well established with my duties, but the challenges for Mina, who at the age of 28 had never been the lady of the house, were many. The house into which we moved was one of a number of homes in Hoechst that had been requisitioned by the Allies, and the maid that came with our house was none other than its owner, Frau Hermann. Frau Hermann was both a joy and a concern in our lives. She had stayed on as a maid to the young military couple for the specific purpose of keeping an eye on her home and furnishings, and thus she was never far behind Mina as she went through her daily chores. On the other hand, she was also an experienced housekeeper and cook who took Mina under her wing, beginning the hands-on training of a young woman who had never cooked a meal in her life, but later would be lauded by friends and family alike as an outstanding homemaker. It was not long before I could compliment Mina on a good meal and mean it, and she was no longer nervous when we began having dinner guests.

30.

ECIC, 1947 - 1948

I HAVE DESCRIBED my time with the European Command Intelligence Center as fairly routine and "not very exciting," but a closer look reveals that our assignments were anything but routine tasks. The Commanding Officer of ECIC put me in charge of the Documents Section, which was primarily responsible for searching for and collecting documents that might prove valuable, in terms of tactical and strategic information to the United States Military. The Cold War with the Soviet Union was just beginning, and special emphasis was placed on culling whatever data could be found regarding Russia's military units, their composition, strength, and armaments.

1st Lt. Peer Herschend was my assistant and, in addition to several enlisted men, there were five American soldiers-turned-civilian Army employees and two German workers in my section. One of the American civilians spent a lot of time in Nuremberg, and another one was almost permanently stationed in Berlin; both were excellent at digging up useful information. The Nuremberg War Crimes trials were drawing to a close, but our Documents Section was still finding and feeding whatever documents we could that would prove helpful to the Allied prosecutors. ECIC was the place where German scientists and other important civilian and German military personnel were interrogated. I learned that one of the German military men who was being questioned at ECIC had grown up in Wuerzburg. Thinking that it might be interesting for Mina to talk to him about what happened in Wuerzburg after she had left, I decided to "check him out" for some hours and then I called Mina to tell her to expect a guest for dinner. And how surprised and even a bit nervous Mina was when the guest, in civilian clothes, was none other than Lieutenant General Fritz Bayerlein, a former Assistant Chief of Staff for German Field Marshall Erwin Rommel. The general, who I knew was strictly a career military man and not a Nazi party product, was very pleasant company. He and Mina had a number of common acquaintances and they reminisced quite a bit. Frau Hermann, whom Mina had asked to stay and serve the meal, became excited and was shaky serving when she found out who our well known guest was. After a good meal and some enjoyable conversation, I took General Bayerlein back to "Camp King."

The work that I described as "not very exciting" also included runs into the Russian occupied Zone of Occupation to follow up leads on useful documents. The Berlin Wall and the fence separating the zones were not up yet, and the occasional "moonlight requisition," against standing orders not to enter that zone, got us what we were after: documents and studies that gave us useful information of military value, as well as documents that were of use at the war crimes trials at Nuremberg. Fortunately, we were never caught.

Besides my duties at ECIC and Mina's responsibilities in our home, we took every opportunity we could to try and discover what had become of the family members we had been forced to leave. Upon first arriving back in Germany, I went right to Drove to inquire about my parents. I had no luck there. The former neighbors I talked with seemed embarrassed by my questions, and could only tell me that the story circulated at the time was that all Jews from Drove had been "resettled." I followed up with the International Red Cross, the United Nations Relief and Rehabilitation Agency, various departments of the Polish government, and the various American relief agencies, all to no avail. I went back to my family home in Drove several times and, assuming ownership of the house would eventually be returned to me, I arranged for repairs to be made to what had been damaged during the war.

Of course, we also traveled to Wuerzburg-Heidingsfeld where we were able to get at least some information concerning Mina's family. Greeted by Mina's former neighbors and landlords, the Becks, we were told that Aunt Hannchen had been moved to an old-age home where she had died, and that Uncle David had been "deported." Mina later found out that her uncle had been deported to Theresienstadt, and lasted six weeks before dying there under brutal conditions. Absolutely nothing was left of the old house the Menko family had lived in for generations. It had been completely destroyed by Allied bombing raids during the war. We visited the grave of Mina's father at the Jewish cemetery while we were there, and then left, promising the Becks we would come back again. We did, several times.

While fraternization with Germans was not forbidden any more, though not encouraged, and even though contacts with Germans would have been easy for Mina and me because we spoke the language, we did not cultivate social contacts with other Germans. Exceptions were made with only a few people in our hometowns where we still knew people who had been loyal and had stayed friends of our families even when it was dangerous for them to do so during the Nazi regime. Social activities for young couples like us consisted almost exclusively of dinners, dances, parties and card games held at the Officers Club or in the homes of other Americans who were living in Germany. Weekends allowed us to take trips, often to Luxemburg or Strasburg, where shopping was not a problem and the stores were full of many things that were not available in Germany. A ten day annual leave took us on one occasion to Switzerland for a nice vacation, and on another one to Copenhagen, Denmark.

Cars were simply impossible to get in Germany, with the Military Exchange Service importing only a few each month from the U.S. and a lottery that determined which lucky American would get one. Our vacation trip to Denmark was actually made to pick up a new Chevrolet which cost $1,800, whose parts supposedly had been shipped overseas and then assembled in Copenhagen. A civilian neighbor who was involved with the "Stars and Stripes" newspaper and obviously had some special connections was able to arrange that purchase for me. I then immediately called a young Air Force officer whom I had met. This fellow was in Germany on a two month long temporary duty assignment and had offered me $1,200 for the Dodge, saying he wanted to see as much as he could of the country in the short time he was going to be there, and would pay any price to get a car. I gladly turned my old Dodge over to him, and adding just $600 to what we got for the 1938 model, Mina and I used a few days of my annual leave and took a train to Copenhagen to pick up our brand new 1948 Chevrolet sedan. We had an interesting experience when we stopped at a street corner and asked someone for directions. Since we were speaking German, three different people stared at us, and without saying a word they moved on. Then I decided to ask for directions in English, and immediately a number of people congregated and were more helpful than we could have hoped for. It was only a few short years after the German occupation of Denmark had ended, and the Danes showed their sentiments. Our objective obtained, we were driving our new car back to Germany, when I decided to make what I thought would be a brief stop in Einbeck. There, Mina and I experienced a pleasant and unexpected surprise.

Mr. Keim, one of the two men who had sneaked across the lines that night to ask our help in saving his city from destruction back in 1945, and whom I then installed as temporary mayor the day after we occupied Einbeck, was still the mayor there! We were directed to his house, where we were heartily welcomed, wined and dined. He then took us to City Hall, where we were introduced to several more officials, and where Mr. Keim thanked me publicly—again and again—for having saved their city. Ironic, when one considers that just two years before we were trying to kill each other! Life for us was full and exciting and, in a short time, would become even more so.

31.

A Family of Three

WE HAD NOT told our families back in Philadelphia that Mina had become pregnant only a few months after her arrival in Germany. Her pregnancy had proceeded without complication, but we had agreed to keep the news to ourselves until the baby was born. Thus it was that on April 11, 1948, Evelyn Ruth Kaufman came into the world at the 97th General Hospital in Frankfurt, without difficulty or fanfare. We were elated with our new daughter; Peter immediately established a protective zone around little Evy. The family in America reveled at the news, and—perhaps for the first time—Mina and I felt the pull to return to our new home and our loved ones in America.

Even as we discussed how and when we might be able to move back, the decision was made for us. The Army had begun a "force reduction" campaign, and I—with my status of limited service—failed my annual physical exam. Although feeling and strength in my arm and hand were continuing to improve, the Army decided I was not up to general active duty. Had we not already been setting our sights for home, this turn of events might have been troubling, but when I received orders saying I was to ship out by mid-December for evaluation at Walter Reed Hospital in Washington, we were quite ready to go.

Once again, Mina and I were leaving Germany. Goodbyes were made, last parties attended, and household goods were crated and sent on their way. Our family left Hoechst with Evy tucked safely into the backseat of the Chevy next to Peter. The trip was quite an adventure, because heavy fog never lifted, and the ride over rutted, bumpy and unrepaired roads took all the control and skill I could muster, until we arrived safely at Bremerhaven. On arrival, we took an unhappy Peter to a kennel, where he was to be crated and held for shipment to the States. After spending the night in officer's billets, Mina in the morning had to join all women who had children for a health check by a nurse prior to boarding the ship for the voyage to the States. A number of women had children of different ages, and when the nurse came to look at little Evy and saw Mina's American passport, she opined that there was at least one "legitimate" American baby in the bunch. Many American soldiers and civilian U.S. government employees had been living with German girlfriends and had not married them because, if they married them, they would have their tours of duty cut short, would have to leave Germany within two months and be returned to the States, either for reassignment or for discharge. Many liked their assignments, and the girls were glad to still be with their families. In 1948 Congress passed a law that, beginning on January 1st, 1949, all "War Brides," women who were citizens of other countries and had married Americans, would fall under the quota system that sometimes would present difficulties and delays for anyone wanting to come to America. Since until the end of 1948 there were no visa restrictions for War Brides to enter the U.S., many couples, including those with children, which included two American civilians in my section, got married and were able to leave Germany as close as possible to the deadline. The ship we were returning on was one of the last ones that would arrive in the U.S. before the end of the year. It arrived at Fort Hamilton in New York after an uneventful voyage on December 24, 1948. Herbert and Rosa were waiting for us on the pier, to take us home.

32.

Serving Stateside, 1949 - 1951

THE REUNION WITH our loved ones, Lotte, Fred and George, Carolyn, and Fanny, Herbert, Rosa and Mother Emma was, to say the least, a happy occasion for Mina and myself. The house on Wagner Avenue overflowed with joy at our homecoming, which was made all the more sweet by the introduction to the family of eight-month-old Evy, who immediately stole the spotlight and the hearts of all who met her.

Having been royally welcomed, we three Kaufmans retreated to Mina's old room on the second floor. After a few days, the household had fairly adjusted to two more adults and a baby in their midst. But, no sooner had things settled down than a howling, very happy, very excited Peter arrived—knocking Mina over, jumping on me and scaring Mother Emma from the room. He growled at anyone who dared go near Evy—and, in general, caused havoc with his exuberance at having been released after weeks of being in a cage and quarantine. A kind distant cousin, Siegfried Schweizer promptly offered to take Peter to his farm for a while, and after a few days the household again returned to a comfortable routine. Just before I shipped out for Europe in 1943, Siegfried had taken Mina and me to a friend of his in Princeton, who told me "Lieutenant, go give them hell." The friend was Albert Einstein. For the next few weeks Mina and I enjoyed the last of my leave visiting friends and relatives, showing off our baby girl, and relishing just being home again.

When my leave finally did come to an end, I reported to Walter Reed Army Hospital in Washington for what I thought would be a short inpatient stay, to be evaluated for fitness for general duty. Several months passed, during which time I was examined and tested, underwent physical therapy, had x-rays and whirlpools, and was examined all over again. During occupational therapy I made some pieces of furniture and some jewelry that I was allowed to take home. Not having any duty assignments, I was able to spend a lot of time with my family in Philadelphia, once my car had arrived from Germany. In due time, a Board of Medical Officers convened and decided that I was physically fit and should be returned to active duty. I always knew that I did not intend to spend my life in the military, but I was also relieved that my service was not to end just yet and that, if needed, my family and I could still avail ourselves of medical care at military medical facilities.

In April, after almost three months at Walter Reed Hospital, I received orders to report without delay to the G-2, the Assistant Chief of Staff for Intelligence, at Headquarters First Army, on Governor's Island, New York.

Once again, the Kaufman family was on the move. U.S First Army controlled a number of houses in Orangeburg, New York, where I was assigned a nice two bedroom house. It was a little place in a friendly neighborhood that was about an hour's drive from work, and where several other officers lived and with whom I would carpool to the Battery in New York, from where we would then take the ferry to Governor's Island. Quarters had been available for our family on Governor's Island, but since no pets were allowed there, the tradeoff for my long daily commute was that one very happy German shepherd could be with his family again. Next, I rented a truck, and an old friend helped me to cart furniture from Mina's bedroom. Household goods that had been in storage since they arrived from Germany were now delivered, and the Kaufman family was resettled again into a life of contented domesticity.

Once into my new position, I decided that my time at Governor's Island was probably going to be remembered as one of the least satisfying assignments of my military career. The work in the Plans and

Training Section was not particularly stimulating, and my Section Chief's micro-managing of the staff made him unpopular with just about everyone. On top of it all, the Chief and I took to one another about as well as oil and water.

I was not a happy camper, but, since I did not plan to make the Army my lifelong career, I was far less worried about my evaluations and efficiency reports than some of the other officers in the Section. I just focused on what needed doing, and made the best of it while I was there. I believe that my chief resented the fact that after less than five years in the Service, I had advanced in rank from Private to Major, while he was only a Lt. Colonel, having entered active duty after Pearl Harbor with a Reserve Commission as Captain.

Despite the frustration and boredom of my job, our family's time in New York was hardly without its bright spots. Mina and I were able to visit frequently with Joe and Ann Blumenthal, and we developed a relationship of deepening affection. Our constant companion, Peter, was bred at Siegfried's request with a pedigreed shepherd named Chici, who promptly graced us with eight puppies, and for several months we found ourselves running a canine nursery in our basement. This had all been unexpected. When I went and picked up Peter, Siegfried had asked me to get a female dog for him so that he then could mate her with Peter and go into the dog breeding business. Since I considered it a favor that the Schweizers had boarded Peter until I could have him back in my own home, I found a well-bred female German shepherd called Chici not far from Orangeburg, bought her and took her to Bound Brook, New Jersey, where Siegfried had his farm. I took Peter there, and the two dogs got together; but my relative had not counted on his wife's reaction. While she had tolerated well-trained and well-behaved Peter while he was at their farm, she had no use for Chici, a kennel dog with imperfect manners. I received a pregnant Chici back and ended up with two big dogs in the house. Then came the litter of puppies, and for more than six weeks the Kaufman's house smelled of disinfectant, that changed only after all but one of the puppies had found homes, and we simply gave Chici back to the kennel where I had purchased her. The one male puppy that we did not give away was called Buster, and in time he became a very important member of our family. Peter, whom Siegfried's wife had not objected to, was once again taken to the farm and lived out his life there, often visited by us.

There was never a dull moment in the Kaufman's lives. About the time the eight puppies were three weeks old, Colonel Meyer, The G-2 of First Army decided to visit some of his officers at Orangeburg, a social visit that can best be described as "checking to see if the host and his family conduct themselves in a manner that befits an Army officer." Included, in addition to politely taking some refreshments offered is often a visit to the kitchen, where the refrigerator evokes attention. During casual conversation, a white gloved hand gently runs over the top, and it had better stay clean, or the hostess gets a stern look. It's the so-called "white glove inspection." We were lucky because all the windows in the house were open, and the puppies were seemingly taking a nap during what turned out to be a very short visit and Mina received an approving gesture when the Colonel and his Lady left the house to visit another Officer.

Best by far was the announcement in the fall of 1949 that Mina was expecting again; our second child was due to arrive in June. And then, right on time and much to her family's delight, Renee Corinne Kaufman came into the world on June 16, 1950, in the military hospital at West Point. While Mina was waiting for Renee's arrival, a lady approached her bed and disappointedly said that she thought her friend Barbara Eisenhower, General Eisenhower's daughter-in-law was still in that bed and had not been discharged yet. Something like this can only happen at West Point!

As if all of this was not enough excitement for us, my Section Chief knew that the young decorated Infantry Major in his section had quite a bit of combat experience and, having been deemed fit for field duty, in his efficiency report he stated that Major Kaufman would no doubt serve his country best with an assignment to a combat unit. Thus it came to pass that, little more than a year since moving to New York, we found ourselves transferred again—this time to the 9th Infantry Training Division at Fort Dix, New Jersey. It meant moving out of our comfortable little house in Orangeburg, New York, and into "barracks living." Our housing in the West End Plaza at Fort Dix was in troop barracks that had been converted into three apartments. When we went to inspect the apartment and opened the door, our four legged companion immediately told us what he thought of the accommodations: there was a pole that supported the ceiling in the middle of the room....

I often said that Mina somehow managed to immediately make each of our living spaces feel comfortable and homey. However a toddler, a newborn, and a young German shepherd probably had a hand in making that process a little more difficult this time around. I was made Executive Officer of the Second Battalion, Sixtieth Infantry Regiment, with duties that were largely administrative. Along with overseeing Supplies and the Company Orderly Rooms, serving on Courts Marshals, and holding inspections, I occasionally took an active leadership role in the twelve-week basic training courses that were running continuously at the base. During one exercise while bivouacking on a cold night, my left arm and hand froze up, making it impossible for me to even hold my pistol. When I stopped in at the base hospital the next day, the examining physician was surprised that I had ever been deemed fit for general duty. In short order I found myself referred to an orthopedic surgeon, who concurred with the hospital physician's findings and, in turn, recommended my medical records be reviewed by a Medical Board, in order to determine the extent of my disability. Remembering a similar experience at Walter Reed Army Hospital, I prepared myself for any outcome.

Around the time I was transferred to Fort Dix, the military situation in Korea came to a head when North Korea launched a surprise attack on South Korea. Demands by the United Nations Security Council to return to their border went unheeded by the Soviet trained North Korean units, and to enforce the U.N. demand, President Truman once more committed U.S. troops to war. Fully expecting to be sent to a combat unit after more conditioning, I was wondering how I, as an infantry officer, could now function under actual combat conditions since I was left-handed and had only limited movement in my left arm. The night training exercise in the Ft. Dix Bivouac area provided the answer.

A three-man Board of Medical Officers convened in December of 1950. After checking all my medical records, and some deliberation, they declared me unfit for military service, and recommended that I be retired for reasons of a physical disability of 40 percent. Orders were published a few days later, making my retirement effective January 31, 1951. We were given thirty days to vacate our quarters, and that was the end of my military service, just a week short of nine years.

I was thirty years old, Mina thirty-one. And while this particular chapter of our lives had ended a bit more abruptly than we expected, both of us had been through much worse before. As it turned out, this was all to have been but a prelude to our next six decades together.

33.

Life Altering Decisions

JANUARY 31, 1951 arrived, and with it came the realization that within a few weeks I would find myself without a job, without a home, with few financial resources, and responsible for a family of four. I had often thought about that possibility, but I was still surprised when it actually came about with the decision of the Medical Evaluation Board at Ft. Dix. I had been in the Army since February 1942, and now there was no future for me in the military service because of my damaged left arm. I had become ineligible even for temporary military service. That physical disability also kept me from going back to the kind of mechanical work I had done before I joined the Army immediately after Pearl Harbor. I had no schooling or training for any business, and the outlook for the future was uncertain. It was reminiscent of May 1939, when I was leaving Germany for this country and also heading into an uncertain future. The difference was that at that time I was single and unencumbered, while now I had the obligations that come with supporting a family.

Denied a chance to become a veterinarian in Germany, when I was expelled from school in 1936 because I was Jewish, I was hoping to someday, some way have a chance to own a farm and work with animals. In 1946, while I was convalescing from injuries and surgery, I used several leaves from the hospital and attended courses in Poultry Husbandry at Rutgers University. At the time I was still hoping—against hope—that my parents had escaped the Holocaust somehow, and I could bring them to this country, to a place where they could recover from the inhumane treatment that they were subjected to during their persecution by the Nazis, and where they could feel secure and keep busy. Unfortunately, they did not survive. They had been murdered in March 1942.

In January 1951, after five more years in uniform, now no longer having to consider a home for my parents, and with little other choice, Mina and I decided to try to buy a poultry farm.

34.

Buying a Farm

FOR MONTHS IN 1949, before I was sent back to duty from Walter Reed Army Hospital, and now while waiting for the Medical Disposition Board at Fort Dix to convene and decide my case, Mina and I had been traveling all over New Jersey, looking at poultry farms that were for sale. We were wondering where we might find one that was affordable, if I should be separated from the Service because of my physical condition. Most of them were simply out of our financial reach. In December 1950, when orders to retire me were issued at Ft. Dix, effective January 31, 1951, they also specified that the government quarters I occupied at Fort Dix had to be vacated within 30 days. The last thing we wanted to do was to move back into Mina's family home in Philadelphia, even if only temporarily.

Fortunately, while at Fort Dix, I had met up with 1st Lt. Jack Arthur, a fellow officer I had served with at ECIC in Oberursel. Jack and his wife lived in Toms River, and when he learned that I was about to be discharged from the Service and was looking for a poultry farm, he invited us for dinner. Other guests at the Arthurs were neighbors of theirs, Dick and Bernice Hartman. Dick happened to be the Ocean County Agricultural Agent and an adjunct professor at Cook College, the Agricultural School of Rutgers University. During dinner, Jack mentioned that we were thinking of buying a poultry farm. Trying to discourage us, Dick began telling us what all was involved in operating a farm. He mentioned that part of his job was visiting poultry farms in the county in order to help farmers solve some of their problems. He found that a lack of basic knowledge and experience was usually the cause of their troubles and their calls to him for advice. Plainly, his well-intended advice was not to buy a poultry farm until I had some working knowledge of farming. I then related that I had grown up in farm country, had even milked cows that my family had kept, and that I had taken the Poultry Short Course at Rutgers University in 1946. A surprised and impressed Dick immediately changed his attitude and offered whatever help he could give. He then mentioned the name of a feed salesman, Clark Inman, who was familiar with a farm that was for sale in New Egypt. When told of our strapped financial situation, he suggested that we look at that farm, and then contact the Farmers Home Administration for financing possibilities. Dick thought that the FHA might help us with the purchase of the farm if they considered that my background and/or experience were up to the task and, if the farm was suitable and the price was right. Mina and I thanked him and appreciated his expert advice.

I called Clark Inman, the local feed salesman for a big feed Company, who made an appointment for us to see the "Applegate Farm," as it was known, on the 23rd of January, 1950. Located about two miles east of New Egypt on well-traveled Route 528, and only a short walking distance from its intersection with Route 539, the farm was easily accessible. Miss Gross, the owner of the farm, was a nice elderly lady who showed us around. The property consisted of 50 acres of rolling farmland, with over 500 feet of highway frontage. There were some 10 wooded acres, about 20 acres suitable for crop growing, and the rest, except for where buildings stood, was hilly grassland, the "Range," over which five 8 by 12-foot brooder hous-es—also used to raise chickens—were spread out. A large corn crib, a tool shed and a cinderblock two-car garage were near the farmhouse. An empty two room bungalow on the far end of the property had wa-ter from a drilled well and electricity, but no indoor toilet. The poultry building, 20 feet wide and 360 feet long, was divided into eight 40 by 20-foot pens, and had a feed and coal storage room located in the middle. The building showed that it had not been used for quite some time, and it was not exactly the ideal chicken house that I had envisioned. I calculated that, after considerable changes and repairs, it could accommodate about 2,000 laying hens.

On April 1, 1864 a mortgage of $ 59.66 had been placed on the farm and home, and it had been satisfied on January 6, 1869. The house was at least that old, and possibly much older.

It had a kitchen that had been added to the original two-story house, a dining room and a living room downstairs, and a bathroom with a sink, tub and toilet between the two bedrooms upstairs. A basement located under the living room and dining room was big enough to hold a water pump and a tank that supplied water to the farmhouse and the poultry building; a storage area and a small, fairly new oil heater that warmed the downstairs part of the house. A small register upstairs in the bathroom floor next to the toilet kept the water lines from freezing, but could not heat the bedrooms. There was no basement, just a crawl space over bare earth under the kitchen, and the house had no insulation in the walls or attic. "Primitive" would have been a complimentary description of the house.

The asking price for farm and house had been reduced to $ 17,000; it was available for immediate occupancy, and Miss Gross was willing to wait until the buyer could secure financing. We thanked Miss Gross for showing us around. On leaving the farm and out of Miss Gross' earshot, an unhappy Mina expressed her feelings: "You are not going to get me to move into that dump!"

That was on the 23rd of January. After a few more days of keeping a baby sitter busy while looking once more for a farm we would like, we came to realize that, considering our financial situation, we could not afford any of the farms we had looked at, and liked. What had made our financial situation difficult was that we did not expect to have to use our nest egg so soon; we had loaned almost all of our savings to Lotte and Fred, who used the money to buy a house. They had started a dry goods business and used the basement of the house for supplies and storage, and at the time were in no position to repay the loan. Upon retirement, my monthly pay of $ 400 plus free housing as a major would shrink to $ 160, based on 40% disability, and there was no more free housing. The quandary we were now in was that, within little more than a month and having very few available funds, we either had to rent a place or find a farm we could buy, secure a mortgage, arrange for a start-up loan, make settlement and be able to move in before we would find ourselves homeless. We had no choice.

Desperate, we went to the Farmers Home Administration office in Freehold, Monmouth County, to find out if we could get help to buy the "Applegate Farm" in New Egypt.

A former Navy veteran, Harry Fenton, was interning at the FHA office in Freehold before he was to move to Toms River to take over the Ocean County office. We discovered that he and I had a lot of interests in common, and we hit it off immediately. Harry described his organization's functions, which included telling us that the FHA was an agency of "Last Resort" for qualifying farmers whose application for loans had been turned down by at least two lending agencies. That would present no problem, I easily assured him. Harry then arranged for me to meet at the farm with him, his chief and a professional appraiser for the FHA. I told him that, if at all possible, and if the FHA approved my application, I was anxious to move directly from Ft. Dix to the farm. Two days later the four of us met at the farm, and after a thorough inspection—the farm house was of the least interest or concern to the FHA people—the consensus was that the price for the farm was reasonable. The FHA representatives felt that, with a lot of work and some changes, the place had many possibilities. It could be made into a nice egg production operation and provide a living for a family. But, first of all, to make it economically viable, the poultry house would have to be enlarged, so that 1,000 more laying hens could be kept there, in addition to the 2,000 that I had estimated the building could hold. Our application was approved after the favorable appraisal, and apprehensively we bought the farm. The FHA would help us with advice as well as a suggested "Farm and Home Plan," and a budget, as soon as we were settled.

Back in the Freehold office, many papers were hurriedly filled out. An application for a mortgage of $ 17,000, and for an operating loan of $3,000 were both contingent on the outcome of a Title Search to prove that there were no liens against the property. Interest payments for the mortgage were at 3 %, and at 3 ½ % for the loan.

To get a Title Search done usually took 30 days or longer, but in my usual "get it done" style I found an attorney who was able to complete it in 10 days. With the search results in hand, I went to Dayton Hopkins, Miss Gross' lawyer in New Egypt, and asked him to make sure that the Deed to the property was ready, so that settlement could be made before the end of the month. His comment was "Major, you are pushing me faster than I can move." The "pushing" helped, and on the 26th of February, with Harry Fenton representing the Farmers Home Administration, we closed the deal on the farm. With newly acquired property, a big mortgage to go with it, and new life-long friends, Harry Fenton and soon also his wife Mary, we made our last move "Courtesy of the U.S. Government" to our farm in New Egypt. We left Ft. Dix on February 28, 1951, the very last of the 30 days we were given to vacate our quarters.

At last, Mina and I and our two little girls had a permanent place we could call our own. And Buster, the girls' constant companion, was able to have an immediate romp in the open space.

35.

Getting Started

AS SOON AS the moving van was unloaded and its contents stowed away in the house, I went to check and see what needed my attention first. I found the buildings contained a lot of useless equipment and realized that the first thing that I needed to get was a pickup truck, not only for cleaning out the buildings, but also for handling the 100-pound bags of chicken feed and other farm supplies. Mina had begun working her magic as soon as Evy and Renee were taken care of. She had started scrubbing the place from top to bottom, but the kitchen floor needed more attention. Ripping out the old oil cloth, thoroughly cleaning the floor under it and laying down the new linoleum was my first work day on the farm. Evy was then allowed to play in the kitchen, Renee was in a playpen in a corner, with Buster watching both of them while stretched out in the doorway between the kitchen and the dining room. In the meantime I had been busy opening a checking account at the local bank, getting telephone service and stopping at the post office to let the postmaster know that we had moved into Plumsted Township. With my shopping privilege at military installations retained, I had also gone to the Ft. Dix Commissary to buy groceries.

Harry had come to discuss the "Farm and Home Plan" with us. The plan consisted of an itemized list of our assets and liabilities; estimates in detail of anticipated living expenses, farm operating expenses, capital expenditures, use of operating loans, crops to be grown, livestock products that could be used, and the debt repayment schedule for a year. We both agreed that we would follow the plan as best we could.

Dick Hartman already knew that we had bought the farm when I called him, and he showed up the day after Harry had been there. Over a cup of coffee he offered much advice, telling me where used equipment for an egg operation was for sale and where I should look for poultry supplies. He also gave me the name of a dairy farmer in New Egypt, Tony Wikswo, who on a share basis might be interested in crop farming the 20 acres of level land. Tony could also keep the grass on the Range area mowed as long as I did not have equipment to do so myself. Dick mentioned it, but I already knew that under the GI Bill I could enroll in courses in poultry husbandry that were being taught at the Freehold High School, 20 miles away. A big incentive was the $ 125 a month which, as a married veteran, I would get for attending evening classes once a week.

With the FHA having to approve almost every step in the process, getting the farm operational was the next order of business. Three thousand one-day-old baby-chicks were ordered from the Schubkegel Hatchery in nearby Lakewood. The first 500 would arrive in three weeks, and the other 2,500 would follow another three weeks later. Equipment to raise the chicks was on the farm. Coal stoves with canopies, or hovers, to keep heat in close and the chicks under them warm were in all the pens and the brooder houses on the hill or Range. Bruce McPherson, a local builder, was hired to modify and enlarge the poultry house that in time would be called Building 1. I bought a truckload of used floor boards that became the roof of the building extension. The boards were cheap because many nails were in them, which I painstakingly spent many hours pulling out before the carpenters were able to use the boards. Bruce and his crew completed enough of the building's extension so that we could put the 500 chicks into a finished pen when they arrived, and the whole job was completed by the time the other 2,500 chicks were delivered three weeks later.

It had taken a lot of hard work, but Kaufman's Poultry Farm was now operational. And I soon discovered that taking off the uniform and putting on dungarees proved a lot harder than I had imagined, and I found out that my injured left arm made manual work much more difficult than I had thought. But, I had made my choice, and there was no turning back. There were hard lessons to be learned, and the first one came when the 500 chicks were about three weeks old. I had gone into the pen and left the door open. Having the run of the farm, Buster followed me, and before I could get him out he had scared the chicks who crowded into a corner, smothering about 50 of them. Keeping coal stoves stoked, putting out feed and keeping the glass jars filled with water were constant tasks, until after about four weeks the birds were big enough to drink out of pans, "waterers," that were filled automatically. Feed in buckets was brought to them on a carrier that, on a track suspended from the ceiling, was pushed from the feed room to the pens, and there I distributed feed with a scoop into metal hoppers. After taking care of stoves and ashes I kept looking for more needed equipment that was for sale. As soon as the two girls were taken care of, and always keeping an eye on them, Mina was often busy keeping glass water jars filled in the pens. I bought metal nests and carted them home, and found a farmer who was glad that I took away used roosts that he wanted out of the way.

As had been done with the first 500 chicks when they arrived, as each of the 2,500 was taken out of the box, a drop of Newcastle vaccine was squirted into one of its eyes (Newcastle disease is an infectious viral disease first discovered in Newcastle, England), the first of several vaccinations it would get while growing up. Taking care of the chicks in the poultry house was easy, but the brooder houses on the hill required much more effort. Several times a day I had to take coal, feed and water to them by truck. It was cumbersome because there was no space for storage in any of them. Weaned from artificial heat and having grown feathers, the birds were let out of the houses to "range" during the day, and they were locked up again after dark to protect them from predators. Raccoons, foxes and owls were a constant threat.

Our daily routine was that I took care of animals and maintenance, and Mina saw to it that both children got proper attention and were never left alone for long. Evy always had fun watching those lively chicks when I took her along to the poultry house. A ride in the truck was another of her pleasures. Renee, when out of the playpen, had a good time with Buster, who let her crawl all over him.

As time went on, the chicks grew nicely and visitors often provided a welcome break in the daily activities. Dick Hartman and Harry Fenton were frequent and welcome visitors, and both often had good advice or suggestions. Close personal friendships developed when Dick soon also brought his wife along. The farmhouse had become more livable due to Mina's talent and with our household goods in place.

Mina's birthday that year, May15th, brought another hard lesson, a learning experience. Conscientiously not only taking care of work with birds and buildings, I was also meticulous with the paperwork. But, I had made a mistake. I had entered a single deposit of $ 125—my GI Bill subsidy—twice in my bank transaction records, and a phone call from the bank informed me that a check for $ 20.01 had bounced, and that there were insufficient funds in the account to pay for fuel oil that had been delivered. Mina's birthday was completely ruined after that phone call, and she began wondering if we could ever make a go of it. The day was saved only when Fred and Lotte came, intending to help Mina celebrate her day. Fred was able to give me $ 25, and I rushed to the bank to cover the deficit. We were barely covering all our expenses and making ends meet with a total income of $ 285 a month.

Mina was stunned and in tears when several days later a letter came from the Blumenthals, whom we of course had kept informed about what we were doing. In the letter was a check for $ 5,000 and a brief message: "We know that you are having a rough time of it and hope this will help. Love, Joe and Ann." I immediately called them, struggling to find the right words to thank them, considering that they had also loaned me the money that was deposited in Cuba when I had hoped to get my parents out of Germany. Even though Joe told me I should not, I insisted on having the money recorded as a second mortgage on the farm. It would provide some security for Joe if Kaufman's Poultry Farm should fail. As comforting and helpful as Joe and Ann's gesture was, I repaid the loan with interest as soon as I was able to get financing from commercial lending sources.

Life got to be a bit less hectic when the chicks were fully feathered and did not need heated quarters any more. I stored the coal stoves in the feed room and installed automatic water fountains, nests and roosts in all the pens, as well as time clocks to control artificial lighting. When the birds were about 18 weeks old, they were vaccinated again both for Newcastle disease, and also to protect them against Fowl Pox. Each bird, after it was caught and vaccinated, and before it was moved into another pen that had been emptied, was "de-beaked," This is a procedure by which, with an electrically heated hot blade a small part of the bird's lower mandible or beak is cut off and cauterized. Being cannibalistic, the birds after that can eat and drink normally, but cannot peck and harm each other. While the birds in the poultry building were distributed and occupied most pens, the birds from the Range were caught, vaccinated, de-beaked, put into crates and carried to the empty pens in the building, filling it to capacity.

The corn that Tony Wikswo had planted on the large field on the hill looked very good, and he had kept the Range mowed whenever it needed it. A few weeks of relative ease were a nice change and gave Mina and me a chance to spend more time with our two girls, and Buster would now also have more freedom, after having been kept from running freely near the Range as long as chickens were out there. We also slowly got to know our neighbors and people in the community.

36.

The First Egg

IN AUGUST, A distant cousin of mine, Fritz Nova and his wife Coleta, who had come to visit, were walking around the Range and they came back to the house with their find: an egg! It was tiny, and hardly larger than a pigeon's egg, but it was the first one of many millions of eggs that over time would be produced at Kaufman's Poultry Farm. Egg production had finally started.

We knew that, during an average laying cycle of twelve to fourteen months, our birds would produce increasingly larger eggs, beginning with "Peewees," that weigh less than 18 ounces per dozen. While eggs in cartons are usually sold and identified by sizes, they are actually weighed and packed accordingly, with a three ounce range within each size. "Small" eggs weigh between 18 and 21 ounces per dozen, "Medium" size range is between 21 and 24, "Large" is from 24 to 27, "Extra Large" from 27 to 30, and eggs are "Jumbo" when a dozen of them weighs more than 30 ounces.

We became painfully aware of egg sizes, because we started weighing eggs individually on one-egg scales and putting them into cases arranged according to size. We had held off buying mechanical equipment for processing eggs as long as we could, concentrating on paying our ever growing feed bills within ten days of delivery in order to take advantage of a 2 percent discount we got for prompt payment. Weighing baskets full of eggs one at a time kept us working until way past midnight for several weeks. Being in the basement of the house, we could easily keep tabs on the children, and 3 year old Evy sometimes "helped" us until bed time. Renee kept busy with toys in her playpen or her crib, and Buster kept her company.

I decided to use what little cash reserve we had left to buy an "Egg Grader," a machine on which eggs, after having been "candled," passed by a light that would show up imperfections inside an egg and cause it to be removed, would be put on a track and from there be automatically transported to individual calibrated scales. The heaviest, Jumbo eggs, would trip the first scale and roll off on a table. That process would continue down to where the smallest ones would roll last onto the table that had six dividers to keep the sizes apart. The machine could handle 1,800 eggs per hour, the equivalent of five 30-dozen cases, and putting the eggs into cases from the table was fast and easy. Since we did not yet have any customers for our eggs, I arranged for a trucker to twice weekly take our eggs to a nearby Farm Market, to be auctioned off. Prices fluctuated all the time, and there was no way of telling what our eggs had sold for until a check for them arrived, usually after two weeks. I could not yet expect payments that would cover our costs of production, because most of our shipments initially consisted of eggs of smaller sizes, but I knew that would change as soon as our hens would begin to lay larger eggs.

It wasn't long before we went through the hen house several times each day and by mid-afternoon had baskets filled with more than two thousand eggs. There was no way we could clean, grade and pack that many eggs by hand. I talked to Dick Hartman, who suggested that I talk to a local poultry farmer, Roger Atkinson, who had chickens, a hatchery, a feed business, and who also sold poultry equipment. I told Roger that Dick Hartman had suggested that I visit him because I needed to buy an "Egg Washer," but could not pay for it immediately. Would Roger trust me, a newcomer and stranger in town, and sell me a washer that I would pay for as soon as I could? The washer was a tub that held a basket full of eggs, had a heating element in the bottom and a pump that bubbled and circulated water around the eggs. "I have one in stock and you'll have it tomorrow, with enough detergent and de-sudser to get you started," was the immediate reply. After that I apologetically told Roger that I could not buy feed from him, because I had already promised to buy feed from Clark Inman, the salesman of another feed company. Roger thought that was only decent and fair. When after a few weeks I was able to pay for the washer, I also took along a cake that Mina had baked. Mrs. Atkinson was visibly pleased and surprised by the unexpected gesture. Dinner, and a game of "Hearts," had the two couples get together often over the years. It is a friendship that has continued to this day and is carried on by the next generation of both families.

With birds in production and doing as well as could be hoped for, and equipment to handle it in place and functioning without problems, we were soon able to cover expenses and even start repaying some of our loans with receipts from egg sales. Although the daily chores made for a long work day, and we could not easily leave the farm very often, we were finally relaxed enough and found some time to spend socially with relatives and old and new friends. Frank Carter, a local day laborer, occasionally helped out when the birds or equipment needed some extra help. A neighbor, Caroline Lewis, baby sat when we were able to get away some evenings.

Although we had many things under control by this time, we were faced with fluctuating egg prices. Egg prices, like those of many other commodities, are determined by supply and demand. Since they are perishable and marketed daily, the wholesale price depends on how many cases of eggs happen to be available for sale that day in New York, where the price is set for the eastern part of the country. Wholesale egg dealers are canvassed by a market reporter as to their inventory, and the daily price is based on the relation between the available supply and the day's anticipated sales. The egg producer has no control over the price he receives from his dealer since he cannot stop the hens from laying eggs, and he must feed them even when sometimes the prices he receives are below his cost of production. I realized that there were two ways in which I could protect myself from the whims of the marketplace. One obvious way was to try to get maximum output of eggs per bird which lowered feed costs, and the other way was to market eggs directly to customers, bypassing both auction and dealer.

I found out that our eggs were never auctioned off at the Farm

Market, and were always put aside for the same buyer who liked the consistency of their quality. I never received more than market price for our eggs, while other lots were often sold at premiums over market. Not satisfied with the existing arrangement, I contacted a dealer who picked up eggs twice weekly at the farm and paid us a penny more per dozen for all larger size eggs. Not having the expense of the trucker and that small premium for the increasing number of cases of eggs every week added up to a nice saving. I was soon able to line up and supply some grocery stores and restaurants in the area, where I was able to get a nice markup over market price. One day Dick Worrell, the milkman—those were the days when bread and milk men were still making house deliveries—told me that his dairy was trying to sell eggs on their milk routes, but that they never sold more than a case of eggs over several days, and he wondered whether their quality was why they did not move. He said: "Why don't you go see my boss? Maybe we can sell some of your eggs."

I promptly put several dozen eggs into boxes and drove to the Sterling Davis Dairy in Wrightstown. I met the manager, William McDaniel, and told him of his milkman's suggestion. When the manager said that he would like to give it a try, I asked if I could get a contract, since it might interfere with my current arrangement with the dealer. Mr. McDaniel answered: "Mr. Kaufman, I'll be glad to give you a contract, but I might as well tell you that there isn't a contract I can't break, if I want to!" The "Contract" began with just a handshake between the two of us, and the dairy began selling Kaufman's eggs. First starting with unmarked dozen cartons, the dairy soon found it profitable to supply egg cartons with its own logo printed on them, and within several years they were selling 65 cases of "Davis Dairy Eggs" every week on their milk routes. Pleased with how many eggs were being sold on their milk routes, Bill McDaniel once told me "You know, your eggs are selling our milk!" What a nice compliment. Kaufman's Poultry Farm was soon able to expand its own wholesale business, delivering eggs to more food stores and restaurants, and the dealer took what we did not sell directly. The "Contract" ended when the dairy went out of business some 17 years later.

37.

Growth and Tragedy

WHILE THE BUSINESS side of our operation was making gradual progress, I had to concern myself with maintaining a steady, even level of egg production. Replacing the flock of birds once they were not "paying for their feed" any more was solved. I rented an empty building across the road in which Milton Foulks, a neighbor, had raised meat chickens. All the necessary equipment was still there and in good condition. Between this building and the brooder houses on the Range, there was enough capacity to raise replacements for the original 3,000 birds. I ordered those chicks so that they would be grown and ready to lay eggs when the present hens' production would not be economical any more, which is usually after about 12-14 months.

The original flock of chickens had been exceptionally busy that first year, their rate of production had decreased less than expected, and I decided to give them a second laying cycle. It is a six to eight week period during which birds had stopped laying eggs, gradually lost their feathers and grew new plumage. An advantage is that they start laying large eggs right away after they molt, and they lay large eggs while the replacement flock's egg size gradually gets larger. The disadvantage is that they will lay fewer than the 220 to 240 eggs each of them produced during that first laying cycle.

After obtaining FHA approval, I had Bruce construct a "summer shelter," a shed type building that was later converted into a regular hen house and eventually became Building 4. The "summer shelter" became home for many old birds that were still producing large eggs while the new young flock's egg size was growing. The birds that were not moved were sold to a dealer.

With the second young flock coming into full production and the "recycled" hens doing well until the fall of 1953, the original egg grader was replaced by one with twice the capacity. With our two little girls growing and needing more attention, and raising a replacement flock while at the same time taking care of the birds in the hen house and processing eggs, the chores became overwhelming. We needed full time help. We had proven ourselves enough for the FHA to stop monitoring our operation, except for visits that became more social in nature. Since I had been repaying operating loans on schedule, I had no difficulty renewing loans as needed. We then hired a young couple and had them move into the then vacant two-room bungalow that in time was upgraded with the addition of another room, and most importantly, a bathroom. The husband was to help me with birds and buildings, and the wife was to help Mina part time with processing eggs.

By the spring of 1954 automatic feeders had been developed and became huge labor savers. From a large storage bin standing outside next to the building, with the ground grain already mixed in, an "all-mash" ration would slide into a hopper in the feed room. An endless chain moved through the bottom of the hopper and in a U-shaped trough moved feed all through the building, replenished as it kept running through the hopper again. All it required was an electric motor and a time clock to start and stop the feeder every few hours. Realizing that it would be quite a time saver, I called Harry Horowitz, who supplied propane gas to our home and farm, and also sold Kitson poultry equipment. A few weeks later, and the Kaufman's hens in Building 1 were eating all-mash feed that an automatic feeder brought to them. All the feed was now blown pneumatically from the delivery truck into the big storage bin. My concern that egg production might suffer after the change in the ration's composition proved to be unfounded.

Dissatisfied with the course material on poultry farming that was taught at the Freehold High School, I felt that attending an evening course several times each month was a waste of my time and I quit after two years. The hard part of this decision was losing the $125 each month, but I also felt that the time had come when I was able to manage without it. It was a situation so much different from when I needed every penny when we first bought the farm!

Many farmers attended the monthly meetings that were held at the Ocean County Agriculture Building and conducted by Dick Hartman as County Agricultural Agent. It was a meeting at which the various specialists, from fruits and vegetable and livestock experts to Home Economists, Soil Conservation Specialists and Farmers Home Administration personnel discussed current problems and answered specific questions posed by individuals. Having attended and enjoyed several meetings I felt were interesting and instructional, I was invited to join the Ocean County Board of Agriculture, of which some years later I became president. One day, Harry Fenton, who had become Assistant County Agent, asked me to bring Mina along to one of the monthly meetings at the County Agricultural Center. He suggested that she might enjoy a special topic that would be discussed by the Home Economist. Shortly after the meeting started, and completely taken by surprise, Mina and I were called on by Chester Tyson, State Administrator for the FHA. Praising the progress the Kaufmans had made in the short time they had been farming, he handed Mina a nice silver platter inscribed:

Ocean County FHA Farm Family of the Year
Ernest and Mina Kaufman
1953

Needless to say, we were overjoyed at receiving this completely unexpected honor, and I thanked Mr. Tyson profusely, telling him that without all the help from the FHA we could never " have made it this far." The local press, including the *New Egypt Press* covered the ceremony with a big spread. Spurred on, we went home to tackle the next project.

Evy had started school again, was now in first grade, and loved it, and little Renee was kept busy accompanying her parents, "helping" them with whatever they were doing. There were short trips to Philadelphia, with both girls asleep in the car on the way home. And, of course, there were many visits to "our" farm by the Menko and Marcus clans. George and Carolyn, who in 1946 had joined Lotte's family, were frequent weekend guests. Mina's brother Herbert had married Shirley Frankel and he introduced her to the farm. A few years later there were two more Menkos when they visited us: the couple's two children, Allyn-Sue and Arthur.

Finding it impracticable and inconvenient to raise baby chicks away from the home farm, a new Building 3 went up early in 1954, to raise chicks in addition to the houses on the Range. The building at Milton's across the road was converted into quarters for egg layers, since grown birds were easier to manage and required less care. Finding and retaining competent help had also become a problem. The original young couple had moved on to another job and was followed by a couple who came from Pennsylvania. Paul had been laid off and was willing to give farm work a try. After nearly a year he and his wife found other jobs more to their liking. For a while it became difficult to find steady farm help, people willing to work six days a week, and, like at most other farms, there was quite a turnover of personnel for several years. Fortunately, Frank Carter could be counted on to help when needed. Business was thriving, but the work was overwhelming, and I decided to make some drastic changes in the operation of the farm.

Only, before I could do anything about my plans for the farm, we were struck by immeasurable sorrow and tragic loss.

Little Evy, who had entered first grade in school, began complaining that she did not feel right. Her stomach hurt and she had a slightly elevated temperature. Multiple visits to the family physician and treatment with antibiotics and other medications did not bring any relief or a diagnosis. When after several weeks her stomach began to enlarge and she seemed to have difficulty breathing, we took her to the Army Hospital at Fort Dix, where an x-ray revealed a large tumor on one kidney. Immediate surgery was recommended. We left for Walter Reed Army Hospital in Washington, D.C. right after Mina's brother Herbert and my sister Lotte took Renee to stay with Grandmother

Emma. I made a quick phone call to Harry Fenton, and asked him if he would keep an eye on the farm.

As soon as we arrived at Walter Reed Hospital, Evy was admitted, examined and prepped for surgery the following morning. She was diagnosed as having a 'Wilm's Tumor." The cancer, named after the German surgeon who first described it, typically develops in the kidneys of otherwise normal small children. After spending a sleepless night at a nearby guesthouse, Mina and I headed back to the hospital, worrying and hoping that the operation would be successful.

Unfortunately, not only was insufficient knowledge available to help our daughter at that time—there was also insufficient attention given to "best practices of confidentiality" by some staff physicians.

The surgery was performed, and as we rode up in the elevator to see Evy, we overheard two doctors who were in the elevator with us talking about the operation that had just been performed on a little girl to remove a Wilm's Tumor. "They should not even have bothered with the operation," one said, since in his opinion "it was hopeless to begin with." Little did they know that they were talking in front of us, about our child.

Hit with such devastating remarks in such an offhand and callous way, Mina and I got off the elevator and were met by Evy's surgeon. He told us that the operation had gone well, and that he felt certain that he had removed all the tumor. He told us that a round of radiation treatment should begin immediately. Very pointedly, he did not venture a prognosis.

Evy remained at Walter Reed Hospital for the next six weeks. She was kept heavily sedated, took radiation in stride and complained little, bearing it "like a trooper." We rented a room nearby, and Mina was at Evy's side every minute the hospital would allow. I pushed our car to the limit, running back and forth to the farm about every other day. I found out that Harry was doing much more than keeping an eye on the farm. Every morning, before he started his regular daily routine, he drove the 20 miles from his home in Beachwood to the farm to see that the workers were doing their jobs, and each afternoon he'd come back and make sure the eggs were processed correctly and that shipments went out. Who could have a better friend!?

Not long after Evy had been taken to the hospital, we received a letter from Ann and Joe Blumenthal, and along with their best wishes for Evy's recovery they had included a check for three thousand dollars, telling us not to spare any effort or expense for her. There are no superlatives that could describe our feelings about their concern and generosity. Fortunately, we did not need the money, because all that could be done for our girl was being done and we returned the check to Ann and Joe when they came to visit Evy. Needless to say, we could never thank them enough! Evy was alert throughout all her treatments, and when one of the many letters she received from her classmates during that time contained a blank page, she was quick to quip: "Oh, that's from Lenny; he can't write."

All that could be done had been done after Evy had received the last radiation treatment, and she was discharged from Walter Reed Hospital. Weak as she was, she was very happy to be home again. She was bedded down on the sofa in the living room, where an air conditioner had been installed, and where she could watch television and the goings on in the house. Faithful companion Buster parked himself next to the couch and stayed there almost constantly, holding perfectly still and licking her hand whenever she patted him. I went to Philadelphia and brought Renee home.

Although the talk was always about getting better and returning to school, Evy became visibly weaker, and was in increasing discomfort. When, after a few weeks at home, the pain surpassed what we could safely treat at home, we took her to the Army Hospital at Fort Dix. There, under heavy sedation, brave little Evy finally succumbed in her three month long fight for life. Evelyn Ruth Kaufman passed away on December 12, 1954, and was laid to rest in Montefiore Cemetery in Philadelphia. Harry and Mary Fenton had a child near her age, and had taken Renee to their home during Evy's last days and kept her until a few days after the funeral. Even with everyone in the family helping her, four year old Renee had a lot of difficult adjusting to do after we picked her up and brought her home again.

Running back and forth between the farm and Washington, I had neglected to give my car proper attention, and shortly after Evy's funeral it gave out and blew a fatal head gasket. I arranged to buy a new car in Trenton and managed to drive my sick car to within a few hundred feet of the Buick dealer's place, where it simply stopped running and had to be towed onto his lot.

38.

Life Continues

AFTER THE TRAGIC losses that we had endured during the Holocaust, we now had faced the most profound loss any parent can suffer—the loss of one's own child. Resilience, however, is a remarkable trait, and there was Renee to love and care for – and the farm, that after all had to provide a living for us. Life had to go on, and Mina and I buried ourselves in whatever activities we could find. Thanks to Harry, the farm had not suffered in spite of our having been absent so much, and keeping my mind occupied, I gave serious thought to expanding again.

At the farm, Mina and I were busier than ever. The Dairy was using more and more eggs, and in order to supply it and our other customers, more production capacity was needed. When I approached the FHA with a request for loans to enlarge Building 3 and to convert Building 4, that was still just a summer shelter into permanent housing for layers, I was told that I had progressed beyond eligibility for FHA's help, and that I should pursue financing elsewhere. Told that Federal Land Bank and Production Credit Associations would be the logical lending agencies for mortgages and operating capital for farm operations, I reluctantly went to the PCA (Production Credit Association's) office in Moorestown that handled loan applications from Ocean County farmers. I was reluctant, because I knew that I could not get the favorable low interest rates I had enjoyed thus far.

Norman Hodnette, the manager of the Moorestown office of "Farm Credit" and Ann Myles, his assistant, had known about Kaufman's Poultry Farm from visits to the area. After a visit to our farm with an appraiser, going over some records, and consultation with the FHA, they recommended approval to their Boards of our application for a mortgage of $60,000 and an initial operating loan of $20,000. The mortgage rate was to be at 5.75 percent interest, the operating loan at 6 percent, with a monthly repayment schedule of principal and interest. Both Boards gave their approval and I got busy.

This time another builder, also named Bruce (Forbes) went to work. Building 3, the Brooder House was enlarged to double its size, so that with it and the coops on the Range a whole replacement flock could now be raised more conveniently. This arrangement worked well for about two years, until the need for more eggs to satisfy our customers forced us to give up raising baby chicks altogether. I decided to buy "ready to lay pullets," sixteen weeks old birds that had their last vaccination as they were being housed in pens they would stay in for their entire laying cycle.

Changing Building 3 and filling it with grown birds that soon would produce eggs gave us a chance to take a welcome breather. There were no birds to take care of any more on the Range, eliminating a lot of work, and the layers at Milton's farm and those in Buildings 1 and 3 produced enough eggs to satisfy the current needs of our customers. We found more time to spend with Renee, and we were more often able to get together with friends. Not having any problems making monthly mortgage and interest payments on time even gave an always worrying Mina peace of mind. Every few months she, Renee and I could take a quick car ride to New York to visit Ann and Joe, and have dinner with them at the Chambertain, a fine French restaurant in the Theatre District. It was always an enjoyable visit, and the Blumenthals were visibly pleased hearing about the progress their "Charge" had been making,

Back at our farm, Sterling Davis Dairy's egg sales mushroomed, and to be able to satisfy them and our other customers' demands, I decided to go ahead and improve Building 4. The "Summer Shelter" had provided little shelter for the "recycled" birds of the earlier flocks, and keeping "waterers" from freezing on cold winter days had me often going through the building with a torch, thawing out the fountains to give the birds a chance to drink. The shelter had done well for us for several years, but I was now ready to prepare it for the planned construction, and for housing in it an ordered young replacement flock that was growing somewhere in Pennsylvania. While converting the building into a year-round laying house, its length was extended to increase its capacity, and wood and insulation material replaced wire to "winterize" the building that would then hold about 3,000 birds. A driveway to make it vehicle accessible in front of its entire length also had to be constructed.

My mechanical aptitude came in handy when we were about to have the truckload of pullets delivered for housing in Building 4. The last things to be done were the installation of a control panel, fuse boxes, time clocks, the running of wires from the control panel to the automatic feeder, to 15 receptacles for heating cables that were to keep water troughs open in winter throughout the length of the house, to two rows of light sockets, spaced 15 feet apart, and then finally, to connect the live wires from a pole outside the building to the control panel inside. The supplies were there, but the electrician was not. When called, his wife told me that he was drunk.

Faced with yet another technical problem, I called my friend Bill Rovin, who had become an electrician, and told him about the unexpected problem I faced. Bill soon showed up at the farm, looked things over, drew up a diagram for me to follow, and when he left, I was on my own. The next morning, as soon as the farm chores were taken care of, I started following Bill's instructions and began wiring and hooking up what needed to be connected. Stopping only briefly for meals, I went at it all day until dark, and after Renee had been put to bed, Mina spent the entire night holding a flashlight, so that I could keep going. There were some quick trips to the house to see that all was right with Renee and Buster, and when daylight came, I was on a ladder, connecting the wires from the utility pole outside to a cable going into the control panel in the building. When I pulled the main switch, all the light bulbs lit up, and the automatic feeder was operational. It was six o'clock in the morning when I picked up my tools and went into the house for breakfast. The truck with the birds arrived at eight o'clock.

By the end of 1955, Kaufman's Poultry Farm, with the birds in Milton Foulks' coop, had grown to about 10,000 laying hens, enough to take care of its customers again, temporarily at least.

Our personal lives were not the same after we lost Evy. The time came when Renee started school and, despite the trauma of having lost her big sister and best friend, she adopted well to Kindergarten and being around children her own age. It was so obvious that she flourished in the company of other children that Mina and I began to question whether it was fair for her to remain an only child. Herbert and Shirley had become proud parents of their son Arthur the year before, and seeing the hope and happiness they displayed with their baby, we did a lot of soul searching, and then decided to put in another order with the stork. To our great joy we received a delivery on July 24, 1956, when Karen Ann Kaufman arrived to join our family.

Karen was born at the Fort Dix Army Hospital, healthy and without complications for either her or Mina. Parents and newborn settled into a new routine, and Renee had a sister again. Cousin Eugene's wife Lotte came from Freeport, L.I. to help out for a few days, and it was not long before Mina was back in the basement, processing eggs with her helper. To make the house more livable, I had Bruce build an 8' by 12' room and a very welcome bathroom with a shower at floor level next to the kitchen. The added room became my office and provided lots of room for the children to play.

When 1957 came, Building 2 also came into being. It was one of the first windowless buildings in the country, located at a right angle to the other buildings. The other three hen houses had windows facing south to give them as much exposure to sunlight as possible during daylight hours, while the windowless building was insulated; walls and ceiling had artificial lighting and mechanical ventilation, therefore not needing southern exposure. It was a completely new concept of housing birds. They were moving freely about two feet above ground, on a slatted wood floor, under which reciprocating cables with attached scrapers would push the droppings into a pit at the end of the building, to a cross-conveyor that took them to the manure spreader. A four feet wide aisle lengthwise divided the 42' wide by 200' long building into two separate sections, each to hold about 4,000 birds. I modified the nests so that as soon as eggs were laid, they would roll on slightly tilted long wire trays towards the center aisle, making for easy egg collection into baskets on a cart being pushed up and down between the two rows of nests. The biggest advantage of this building was that I could house more birds on a slatted floor because there would be no accumulation of droppings, and there was no need for litter and nesting material.

With birds, lights, big capacity fans and feeders depending on electricity in a closed building, an emergency generator had to be installed. I hooked up a practically new 10 Kw U.S. Army surplus generator, making sure that in case of a power outage our birds in the windowless house would not suffocate.

Since it was the very first such building in New Jersey, I received a lot of help and advice not only from my friends Dick Hartman and Harry Fenton, but also from Professor Wabon C. Krueger, the Rutgers University Agricultural Engineer. "Krueg" had figured out what capacity fans were needed to give each bird enough air to be comfortable, and he also made many good suggestions during the construction period. He would never leave a visit to Ocean County farms without stopping for a chat with me on his way home.

Being one of the few in the country, the building drew a lot of interest in the poultry industry. Harry Horowitz, who had supplied a lot of the equipment for the building, suggested that we hold an "open house" to showcase our building to the poultry farming community. I was skeptical, and dubious. We had worked hard to maintain health standards, and we kept visitors away from our buildings, cognizant of the many diseases, airborne or tracked in by humans, that could be devastating to a farm that now housed 18,000 birds. Harry was convinced that an open house might be good for business, and Krueg was enthusiastic from an academic point of view, suggesting that any visitors going into the building would be asked to simply first step into a pan containing a disinfectant solution. I finally gave in.

The Open House was advertised in "The Poultryman," a New Jersey trade paper published in Vineland, and in some of the local newspapers. And they came. On a nice warm spring day in 1958, Kaufman's Poultry Farm suddenly took on the look of a large county fair, and almost 100 vehicles, with both local and out-of-state license plates, were vying for a parking place. Dick Hartman, Harry Fenton, Professor Krueger, John Bezpa, Rutgers University's Poultry Specialist, and I spent the time playing hosts to the many visitors and answering questions: questions about construction, efficiency, production, and of course most importantly, about costs. Harry Horowitz's company, H & H, provided food and drinks for the crowd that included representatives of the local press as well as of several national poultry publications. The "show" lasted for over four hours, and when the last visitors had left, all of us and our helpers sat down to refreshments Mina had prepared, and we discussed the day's happenings. It had turned out to be a complete success, everybody agreed, and subsequent articles in the press were very complimentary. It had been an exhausting day, but a satisfying one.

At this time, egg production was at an all-time high. My aim was to obtain and maintain an average farm production of better than 65%, which meant collecting and processing more than 11,000 eggs each day. The challenge was to arrange replacement of individual flocks so that the output of eggs of the most desirable sizes remained fairly constant. By ordering replacement flocks for each building to arrive about two to three months apart, I was able to keep my birds and desired egg sizes always through their most profitable period of production before selling them and readying pens for the next flocks.

The excitement around Building 2 was slowing down, and I busied myself with fine-tuning operations on the farm. There was "culling" of unproductive birds—which I had learned to recognize—who then spent time in a separate pen until they went to the butcher with the next whole flock that was being replaced. There was always some mortality among so many birds kept in such close proximity to each other, and birds that had died were incinerated to prevent the spread of anything that might have killed them. Occasionally, when I saw birds that looked diseased, I would take them to the Poultry Pathology Laboratory at Rutgers University, where Dr. Dave Tudor would provide answers to the birds' problems and make his appropriate comments or recommendations.

In addition to paying attention to our birds' health, there was always a need to replace, adjust, repair or tweak a piece of equipment that tested my aptitude. And there were always existing customers to satisfy, and time spent to solicit and make deliveries to new ones. It was a comfortable daily routine and it gave us time to relax a bit and devote more time to our children, friends and family.

In 1959, our neighbor Milton Foulks told us that he and his wife Elizabeth had decided to sell their property and move away, to a senior community. The ranch house, nestled in over ten acres of wooded land, and immediately surrounded by tall oak trees, was a strong temptation for us, and we were already renting and using their coop. There was a drawback, however, and that was that the house had only one bedroom, and we were a family of four. On the other hand, we had always admired the custom built house and its settings, and vacating our old farmhouse directly across the road would provide living space for the additional farm help we had contemplated hiring. A trip to PCA in Moortestown was the next move. Considering our track record, the PCA's president felt we could afford to buy the Foulks property, and that the PCA board would approve a loan for adding rooms to the house and enlarging the poultry building. There were phone calls to the other directors, and the loan was approved. With Milton willing to hold a sizeable mortgage, we became the owners of the Foulks house and grounds.

I drew a diagram of the house we had just bought, and laid out plans that would increase its size by nearly one half, and also enhance its outer appearance. Bruce Forbes was available, and by the time he and his crew were done, two bedrooms and a bathroom had been added to the house that now had three bedrooms, kitchen, den, living room, a small dining room, two bathrooms and a detached garage. I was the electrician for the job. When he was finished with the living quarters, Bruce then enlarged the poultry house enough to accommodate 2,000 laying hens. Bulk feed bin and automatic feeders had by then become standard equipment..

Moving day was almost exactly nine years after we had left Fort

Dix, and for the first time we had a modern home that we could furnish to our taste. The house became the beloved home of our family for the next 40 years, with walls adorned with pictures that were mostly gifts from Ann and Joe Blumenthal.

I found and hired an experienced worker who turned out to be one of my more dependable hands, and Harold Bubb and his family moved into the old farmhouse. Egg processing continued unaffected, in the basement.

Meanwhile, outside activities began to occupy more of my time. Having become president of the Ocean County Board of Agriculture and a director of Farm Credit (FHA) In Moorestown, I was asked to fill the unexpired term of a member of the New Egypt Board of Education. When I stated that I did not consider myself qualified, I was told that I was needed as a business representative on the Board. Persuaded to join the Board, I served out the unexpired term, and was reelected for a new 4-year term. After going through some construction projects at the school at the time, and simply not feeling qualified and adequate to the task, especially concerning academic topics, I decided not to stand for election again once my term was over. At Bill McDaniel's suggestion, I became a member of AUSA, the Association of the United States Army. It is a civilian organization of business and professional people and politicians who support the Military and are one of its main connections with local communities. At dinner meetings several times a year at the Officers Club at Fort Dix, members of AUSA met with the ranking officers of the Fort and discussed current local and national problems and conditions, while at the same time also often developing personal friendships. I had been a member of the Officers Club at Fort Dix when I was stationed there in 1950 and had retained my membership. The club was a convenient place for an occasional dinner with the children, and Mina and I had become acquainted with several officers who also attended AUSA meetings. What resulted were many invitations for enjoyable visits and dinners back and forth between New Egypt and Fort Dix. I was "outranked" almost all the time by our male officer friends, whose age was closer to my own, and Mina became a huge success with her culinary expertise, so much so that invitations to her dinner parties were openly sought after.

39.

The Feed Mill

ONE DAY EARLY in 1962 George Hessenthaler, the big feed company's area salesman who had succeeded Clark Inman, told me that his company would soon discontinue delivering feed to its customers in New Jersey. He stated that there were too few of them left, and it was not worth maintaining their warehouse in Jamesburg, N.J. from where deliveries were being made. He sounded rather disappointed and said that he wished he could keep a good customer like Kaufman's Poultry Farm that had been such a steady customer for over ten years, but there was just no way. Thinking of how advantageous and economical making my own feed could be for my operation, I was quick with an answer: "There is a way for your company to keep me as a customer," I told him. "Your company can finance a feed mill on my farm for me, and you can then sell me freight car loads of feed concentrate that I can unload at the railroad siding here in New Egypt."

Expecting to be told the date of my final delivery of feed, and ready to contact a local feed dealer, I was surprised when after a few days George appeared with Roger Morrison, the manager of the large national company's feed manufacturing plant near Harrisburg, Pennsylvania. I was even more surprised when Mr. Morrison told me that they would love to retain me as a customer and would be willing to finance a feed mill for me. He said that he knew of a reliable company in Lancaster County that had built some small feed mills on farms in the area. He was certain that I could get an estimate from that company of how much a turn-key installation, large enough to keep 100,000 birds fed —my goal—would cost, and he gave me the phone number of a Mr. Herr. He also mentioned that the 6 year old truck with the pneumatic blower that his company was using to deliver feed out of the Jamesburg warehouse and several conveyors, needed to unload freight cars at the railroad siding, could be included in the financing arrangement, since his company would have no further need for them.

Shortly after my phone call Mr. Herr arrived at our farm and, after looking around, he noted that part of the existing corn crib was an ideal location for a small feed mill. He told me that he was able to get a used 65 feet tall grain elevator, a hammer mill with a 50 hp. motor (to grind grain) and a mixer from a discontinued operation, all in good, serviceable condition, at what he expected to be a reasonable price. With his experienced crew, the installation of equipment and the building of all the necessary metal holding bins for different ingredients could be done in about four weeks.

A few days later Mr. Herr was back with a diagram of lay-out and construction details that he had submitted for approval to the feed company's office. They were willing to finance the $12,500 that the feed mill would cost, if I was willing to go ahead with the project. A chattel mortgage form that detailed every item concerning the mill construction and its cost, and listed an additional amount of $3,000 for the truck was promptly completed. Total cost to be financed was $15,500 at 6% interest, payable in monthly installments over a period of three years. We signed the papers, and two weeks later Mr. Herr with crew, equipment and material went to work. The power company installed a separate, heavier service, needed to run the big motors of hammer mill and mixer, as soon as the necessary 400 Ampere control panel was installed.

Mr. Herr's estimate of construction time was correct, and when four weeks were up, we had a feed mill that was operational. The only ingredients that had to be handled manually and would be stored in a corner of the corn crib were bags of calcium or ground oyster shells. They were a needed part of the ration to replenish the calcium that hens consume to make egg shells.

I had spoken to Tony Wikswo and some other farmers in the area who grew corn, the main ingredient in my chicken's feed, and arranged to buy their crops at harvest time. It was an arrangement beneficial for them because of the short distance from their farms to a scale and then to my mill; they did not have to store the corn, and they could make their deliveries at times convenient for them. The advantage for me was that I could eliminate a broker part of the year and save money by buying at harvest time directly from farmers as much corn as I could store.

George Hessenthaler was happy with the first order of feed concentrate I gave him and placed it for the 12-plus ton rail shipment, to arrive soon after the mill was ready. He told me that he had ordered the mix in crumble form, rather than in meal form, because it would flow better and be so much easier to shovel out of the hopper rail car it would come in. Tony Wikswo was the first to bring several loads of corn that he had dried artificially to where it contained less than 16% moisture (Shelled corn will clump up, ferment and stick to bin walls when its moisture content is higher than 16 percent, making it difficult to handle). The elevator worked fine, the hammer mill ground the corn nicely and the corn meal ended up in one of the holding bins. The feed truck had come from Jamesburg with the needed cross conveyor and elevator, and when the freight car arrived, two helpers and I were ready. With electric power to run the motors "borrowed" from the hardware store next to the railroad siding that was about two miles from the farm, it took four round trips to empty the hopper car, shovel the concentrate into the elevator pit at the farm and dump it into the two holding bins intended for it. Unwieldy, especially when moving between buildings at the farm, the big truck was not easy to handle, but it served its purpose well. Pleased with the way everything was working out, I started making feed, always mixing two tons at a time and taking it to where it was needed. It took close to two hours to mix and deliver a batch. Getting used to connecting and disconnecting flexible pipes between truck outlet and bin intake, and then putting the blower motor to work was easy. Above all, I expected my feed costs that I always calculated to within fractions of cents per dozen of eggs produced, to go down quite a bit.

Two weeks later, I suddenly noticed a drastic drop in egg production across the entire farm. I did not find any dead birds or notice any sick ones. There were no problems with time clocks controlling lights or automatic feeders, and water fountains functioned properly. I was the only one who had made feed, and I was sure that I had not made any mistakes. In a short time farm average egg production was down more than one third and I was panicky. I took several birds to Dr. Dave Tudor at Rutgers. Dave did pathology on the birds and found enlarged, fatty livers on all of them, but no disease. "Could there be something wrong with the feed?" was his polite question, knowing that I had just begun operating my new feed mill. He had no definite answers. I went home, worried about how I could continue to supply our customers and pay our bills, because our flocks' production was not covering costs any more. There was no way of keeping my concerns from Mina, since she was aware of the reduced number of eggs she was handling, and she worried with me. I went on and on, searching through the hen houses, looking for an answer—and finally found it. Dave's guess had been right. The birds were not getting the right nutrition. Though the feed was properly mixed, as the chain took it out of the filled hoppers through the pens, I saw that the chickens in the first pens would pick out all the crumbles of concentrate that had not broken down into meal form and mixed with the other ingredients, and the birds in the farther pens got nothing but corn meal and calcium. The concentrate should have been in meal form that mixes easily with corn meal, instead of in crumbles. George's apology and a phone call to Harrisburg got no reply from Mr. Morrison. Aggravated, I got statements from poultry nutritionists at four different State Universities, and every one of them agreed that what I described was happening on my farm would cause the liver problems and loss of production. I thought of suing the feed company, but decided not to, considering that they had a lien on the feed mill and I was in no position to repay them right away. I had to use up whatever crumbles were in the bins and ordered the next shipment with the same ingredients, but now in meal form. By running the automatic feeders after dark sometimes, I was able to get some crumbles also to the birds in the far pens, thereby stabilizing egg production that never returned to a normal level from the affected flocks. Until replacement flocks later took up the slack in production, I had to buy eggs from Roger Atkinson and some other farmers at times to keep our customers supplied. I was granted a temporary extension of the monthly payments due on mortgage and operating loans from Farm Credit, and we were forced to "tighten our belts" for quite some time. We were staring at bankruptcy with debts to the tune of over $ 125,000. There were the mortgages on the farm and on Milton's property, the lien on the feed mill, outstanding operating loans, replacement birds that had to be paid for, and then there were the usual living expenses. We muddled through a year that was tough both emotionally and physically, but we made it. I kept buying feed from the same feed company until the loan for the construction of the feed mill was paid in full, and the recorded lien on it had been cancelled. I then promptly notified the Company that I would no longer buy any feed from them and would not pay the $20,000 that I owed on the last carloads of concentrate, because their salesman's error of judgment three years ago had caused us severe economic losses. I never heard from the big feed company again. Roger Atkinson had retired and stopped selling feed. Agway, a local feed company was glad we became its customer and supplied us as long as we were in business.

In the meantime, the next flocks of chickens were doing well, the customers were satisfied, and I was glad to have the feed mill, because it lowered our feed costs considerably. That was especially helpful at times when wholesale egg prices quoted were low and sometimes even below our cost of production.

In those days Kaufman's Poultry Farm had a lot of visitors from foreign countries. Whenever agricultural delegations came to the United Nations Headquarters in New York and wanted to see farm operations, they invariably ended up at Rutgers University, from where they would then be taken to different types of farms throughout the State. To see a progressive poultry farm they almost always ended up at Kaufman's farm on Lakewood Road in New Egypt, accompanied by guides from the university. I recall that representatives from almost forty different countries had visited our farm over the years.

I sometimes did the grocery shopping for the family at the Ft. Dix Military Commissary, and whenever I went past the display of eggs in the dairy department, I wondered whether there could not be a chance for me to sell my eggs there as well. The close proximity to my farm, a distance of about 8 miles, would present a great opportunity to get "hen-house-fresh" eggs to the shoppers in the store. In conversations with friends in the Military and members of AUSA I was encouraged to contact the officer in charge of the Commissary with an offer to sell my "Fresher by Miles" locally produced eggs. When I contacted him, the Commissary Officer was willing to give my eggs a try, provided my facilities for handling food were approved by the Fort's Veterinary Officer who was responsible for the inspection of all food items that came to Fort Dix.

A visit to the veterinary clinic followed, and an appointment was made to have Kaufman's Poultry Farm's egg processing facilities inspected. A three man team came as arranged. They enjoyed being shown around the farm, and then came to the basement of the old farm house to inspect the "facilities." Utter disaster! While there was no problem with the way the eggs were handled, the ladies doing the work were not wearing head coverings; the old field stone basement walls could not be kept clean or washed down; the water supply had not been tested, and there was no certificate of inspection by the County Board of Health. The obvious verdict: completely unsatisfactory conditions and facilities! So much for getting our eggs for sale into the Ft. Dix Commissary at that time!

I was not surprised that my basement egg room was found unacceptable, but it still irked me, and I was determined to make the necessary corrections as soon as I could. It meant putting up a completely new building and installing the most modern equipment available before I could make another attempt to get the Ft. Dix account. It had taken more than two years for us to survive and recover from the feed fiasco, to catch up and again meet all our financial obligations on time. Getting a loan from PCA to finance such a building therefore presented no problem. I spent many evening hours drawing up plans for an egg processing plant that had to be as labor-efficient as possible, and large enough to accommodate the daily egg production of as many as 100,000 birds, my distant goal. I had ideas of making changes to the existing hen houses that would enable me to increase our bird population and wanted to be prepared, should I ever have the opportunity to supply, if not the Ft. Dix Commissary, any other large volume customers or food markets.

When I felt comfortable with my design and detailed plans for room layout and the locations for equipment to be installed in a 2-story building, I asked Dick Hartman and Professor Krueger for comments or suggestions. I wanted to make sure I had not overlooked anything important for an up-to-date egg processing plant. They both liked the plans, offered few suggestions, and I did what I had done several times before: I made a trip to PCA to arrange financing, and then a phone call to Bruce Forbes to get him to construct the building.

To provide easy access to the plant for cars and trucks from the road, I located the building at a spot where the highway that passed by the farm had been artificially built up and was nearly 10 feet higher than my adjoining pasture land. By erecting the building about thirty feet away from the road, filling in that space with gravel and then covering it with asphalt, I was able to create necessary parking places at road level, and at the same time have a basement that I could easily access from the farm at ground level. Part of the upper floor, the processing area was covered with two inches of reinforced concrete and had to be smooth and impervious to water to facilitate thorough cleaning, while the rest of it, consisting of in-cooler, holding room, freezer, breaking room, office, rest room and stairs to the basement had plain wooden flooring. A conveyor would bring supplies from the basement to the processing area, and the farm house well would supply the water.

The building went up, all refrigeration equipment was installed, and a new egg grader with on-line washer arrived. With a suction device picking up 36 eggs at a time, an operator gently placed them on six eggs wide parallel rollers that moved the eggs through an in-line washer, through the candling booth, and from there to the grader. The person standing in a candling booth would pick out all eggs that were not suitable for sale in individual cartons. Three people at the grader table would put the eggs into cartons, the sizes differentiated by color, and a belt would move them through a closer to a rotating round table, from where they were manually picked up and put into cases. Stacked on dollies, the filled cases were taken into the "out-cooler," or holding room, to await shipment. Eggs coming out of the hen houses were held in the "in-cooler" until they were processed.

Kaufman's Poultry Farm now had an egg processing plant that was promptly approved as being "satisfactory" by the local Board of Health, the County Board of Health, by the Fort Dix veterinary officer and the State of New Jersey Board of Agriculture. That board's approval authorized us to advertise our eggs with something like the "State Seal of Quality" logo printed on our own egg cartons that I was about to order. After a visit to the farm, Milton Dunk, the editor of the "Poultry Tribune," the nation's main poultry industry publication, wrote a very complimentary article about the plant, illustrated it with many pictures and captioned it "Designed for efficiency."

Moving out of the farm house basement required a lot of changes in the processing routine. Instead of Mina and one helper spending many hours daily washing, candling and packing eggs, it took more people now to operate the new, more efficient and faster equipment. The problem of adequate help was solved very easily. Several young local women were glad to be able to work a few hours a day while their children were at school, and Mina had no trouble arranging the schedule to accommodate them. That situation changed later, when more eggs took more hours to be processed, but at no time did Mina ever have to worry about having enough help. If any of the women had to leave for some reason, they always managed to find and recommend someone to replace them or to substitute for them. Mina was a popular "boss."

40.

Raising the Roof

NOW THAT WE had a processing plant which could easily handle the egg production of as many as 100,000 birds on a daily basis, and a feed mill capable of feeding that many, the next project obviously was to get more eggs to sell, and customers to buy them. I tested the waters at Ft. Dix by selling several cases of eggs to the Officers Club and had no difficulty getting them inspected and passed by the veterinary crew. A visit to the Commissary Officer resulted in an order for ten cases of large eggs, a trial order to find out how our eggs would be accepted by the store's customers. The eggs were cool enough, but the van that delivered them was not equipped with a refrigeration unit, and only by protesting that my eggs had the proper temperature when they left the farm, only 8 miles away, and could hardly have warmed up in the less than 30 minutes it took me to get to the Base, did the veterinary inspectors accept them. Kaufmans' eggs disappeared very quickly, and it became a problem for me from then on, because I could make only token shipments to the store until I had more eggs to sell.

Never really pleased with Building 1 ever since we bought the farm, I used money I had received from selling some restituted family property in Germany, and with additional available help from Farm Credit, I kept Bruce busy. I called Frank Myronchuck, a local house mover, to actually raise the roof of the building. I planned to convert it into another windowless poultry house similar to Building

2. However, the egg collection would be different: the nests would hang, back to back, on a wall that split the building into two sections, and have a wide lid covered metal trough in the front into which eggs would roll, ending up on a jute belt. The cover would keep chickens entering the nest from damaging eggs that would already be on the belt. A person standing at one of the two mechanical egg collectors in a small storage room near the entrance to the building would turn on an electric motor, and the endless belts in front of three tiers of nests would bring the eggs from the entire length of the building, from over 300 feet away, to a table for easy gathering. The purpose of all this would be to increase the building's capacity to where it could house about 16,000 birds instead of 3,000.

Frank Myronchuck arrived with jacks, beams and blocks and raised the roof, half of the building at a time. Bruce took care of a footing, so that support beams for the slats could rest on them, and then assembled and erected 10 by 12 feet sections of siding. The frames went up, and after new, taller roof support posts had been put into place, the roof came down gently and was fastened to walls and posts. Once the second half of the building was also done, I did whatever electrical wiring and hookups were needed, and changes that had to be made to the water lines. What was also needed, however, was a larger emergency generator, because the 10-Kw one that I had bought when we built Building 2 was no longer adequate. A brooder house from the Range was moved to a central part of the farm and modified, and a 35-Kw generator was installed in it. This time Raymond Grant, a neighbor who was a licensed electrician and who had made all the feed mill hookups made all the intricate connections from the outside source of power to the generator and from there to all the buildings on the farm. A 500-gallon fuel tank was buried in the ground next to the shed, and a line from it fed directly into the engine that, when running, would consume 6.5 gallons of fuel each hour. A hand crank fuel pump was also attached to the tank, and all vehicles on the farm, cars, trucks and tractors could "gas up" there.

We were able to undertake these and other future projects within such a short period of time for one simple reason: after evaluating our farm operation and considering the progress we had made, the PCA extended us an open line of credit of $100,000.

Birds soon filled Building 1 to capacity, and with the increased egg production Mina and her helpers spent more hours in the processing plant. Until that time she had been doing all the candling and getting orders ready, answering phone calls and keeping equipment running smoothly. Being called away from the booth too often forced her to always stop the machine. She hired an experienced "Egg Candler" to replace her in the candling booth. While shipments to the dairy had leveled off over time, our eggs gradually required more shelf space at the Ft. Dix Commissary, and conscientious, worry prone Mina always anxiously waited for the big truck to come back empty, meaning that the "Vets" had not found any problems while candling 100-egg samples randomly picked from the truck.

Only once was a shipment rejected by the "Vets" during the many years in which we sold eggs to what had become our largest customer. On a Saturday morning, the day before Easter, I was called and asked to speed up the scheduled delivery because the store was running out of eggs. In order to take as many eggs as I could, I included eggs that had been laid and processed that same morning and simply were not cooled down to the required minimum temperature of 60 degrees. Stopping as usual at the veterinary clinic for inspection before driving to the store, the random sample happened to be a case of medium size eggs that had most likely been laid less than three hours earlier. While the rest of the shipment was not sampled and approved, I had to leave 10 cases of medium size egg on the truck and take them back with me, because they did not meet temperature specifications. Back on the farm, I put them into the cooler for two hours and then went back with them to Fort Dix, where the Vets passed and accepted the same lot of eggs that they had rejected when they were three hours fresher.

Renee and even Karen were of much help by then. They helped their mother in the egg processing plant, and their father with gathering eggs when some of the regular employees had their days off or were on vacation. As they grew up they would "punch a time clock" like everybody else and get paid for their work. Even though they sometimes were asked to do chores that were unpleasant, they never complained – at least not to their parents.

Another operation took place in the "Breaking Room," where all stainless tools and equipment were kept immaculately clean and sanitized after every use, because eggs broken out of their shells were involved. Eggs that were not fit to go into cartons or cases, mostly those whose shells were cracked, but whose inner membrane was still intact, as well as misshapen ones and hard to sell small sized eggs were salvaged this way. Homogenized with a big mixer in a stainless container, the liquid would be poured into 30 pound cans and then placed in to the freezer. Bakeries use liquid measure and containers when handling eggs, and it is claimed that the longer they are frozen, the more viscous they become, and the better they are for cake mixes. Frozen eggs that were kept in the freezer for at least 30 to 90 days, and then sold to bakeries were a nice way to make use of what would otherwise have been quite a loss.

Even with egg production from nearly 30,000 birds I was not able to deliver as many eggs to Ft. Dix as the store could use. By using only my own farm production and keeping my price competitive with the other vendors who were mostly dealers and not egg producers, the customers soon found out that Kaufman's "fresher by miles" eggs were just that, and therefore more desirable. Dealers collecting and packing eggs from different farms could not match the uniformity and quality of those locally produced.

My objective to become the sole supplier of locally produced eggs at Fort Dix and to be able to satisfy a growing number of restaurants and grocery stores that had become customers required the addition of still more birds. Compared to the two windowless buildings that had slatted floors and were working out very well, Buildings 3 and 4 were inefficient floor operations. They did not lend themselves to the type of structural changes that increased bird housing in Buildings 1 and 2. There was another way to add more laying hens to the farm without putting up additional buildings: Cages! By making the necessary changes inside the buildings, I figured that I could put close to 15,000 birds into them, compared to the 3,000 each was holding. Plans soon became reality. Not to upset the flock replacement schedule that had become quite a problem by then, I first just tackled Building 3. A crew from New Holland, Pennsylvania, came and did the complete installation of cages, feeders, water fountains, exhaust fans and whatever else was needed. With the crew's job done, there would be three rows of cages, hung back to back and two tiers high through the length of the building, with aisles separating them in which egg collection carts could be moved. Bruce had constructed concrete pits under the cages into which droppings would fall and which, mixed with water would then end up in a tank outside the building. There, a tractor with an attached pump, hose and "honey wagon" would empty the tank and fertilize not only the crop field on our farm, but also some neighboring farmers' fields. Soon, over 7,000 birds were laying eggs in Building 3.

Before converting Building 4 in the same way as Building 3, I found myself too stretched physically, with supervising the farm, making feed and deliveries, and looking up customers. Harold, who lived in the old farm house, and Kenny, the other hired man who lived in the bungalow, often needed help, especially when there were problems with equipment. They were busy not only gathering eggs, but also keeping water fountains clean and automatic feeder hoppers filled, and walking through the pens picking up eggs that had been dropped on the floor by some chickens who did not make it into a nest in time. Frank Carter and Charlie Moore, a local day laborer who sometimes used to help out, were not often available any more, and I was glad to find some High School students who could do some of the chores and help out mostly on weekends. They made getting the work done easier for the Kaufman family members, all four of whom pitched in where necessary. Another full time employee was needed.

Frank Myronchuck had been buying and selling so-called emergency housing that had been built in northern New Jersey shortly after World War II ended, for university students who attended college in New York under the GI Bill. Those houses were now being auctioned or sold off. Frank had moved several of such houses into New Egypt, and I was impressed with the way they looked. Most of them had two bedrooms, living room, kitchen and bathroom, all in about 1,000 sq. feet of floor space. For $2,400 Frank moved one of the houses to a lot next to the driveway to the farm after a foundation had been laid. Utilities were connected and a local used furniture dealer supplied what was needed to furnish the house. And when everything was in place, it took no time at all for a young local couple to move in. The man would work on the farm, while his wife worked elsewhere. Once Bill, the new man was broken in, I went ahead with my plans for Building 4.

With three men now to help, I figured that, even if it would take some time, with my crew I could assemble and hang the cages, install feeders, exhaust fans and water fountains and save on some of the costs. As soon as the building was cleared and cleaned out after the last flock of birds in it had done its job and been sold, Bruce and his men did to this building what they had done earlier in Building 3, and I ordered the equipment.

A huge truckload of precut galvanized wire sections arrived, and as soon as a number of cages were assembled, we would hang them above the pits, suspended from beams under the roof. It took nearly a month until with "spare time work" all the cages were crimped together and hung. Then it took another two weeks to install feeders, fans and water fountains. While the feeders were similar to those used in the other buildings, drinking fountains for caged birds were completely different. A grey plastic pipe fastened to the front of the cages had small red cup-like fountains attached to it, and they were spaced so that there was one cup in front of each cage. The birds would peck on a little float in the cup, and by doing so make it automatically fill with water. When the building was finished and the ordered birds arrived, Kaufman's Poultry Farm had housing for about 45,000 birds.

Having retired and phased out his business, Roger Atkinson during a visit to the Kaufmans mentioned that he was going to sell his bulk-feed truck, and I immediately bought it. It was just large enough to hold the two-ton batches of feed that I was always mixing. Since instead of getting and unloading railroad carloads of concentrate and bringing it to the farm, I was now having it delivered. I had no more need for the big truck and I sold it, because the smaller truck would be ideal for my use. Taking feed to the various bins on the farm became a lot easier.

I had run and buried separate water lines to each of our four poultry buildings, and Vineland Poultry Laboratories, that had supplied the vaccines and medications we used on our farm over the years, had developed a "Proportioner" for adding liquid vaccines or medications to the chickens' drinking water. They were looking for a farm where they could conduct tests under normal operating conditions, and their salesmen knew from visiting our farm that each of our buildings' water lines could be treated individually. Thinking that this layout was ideal for their purposes, one of the Laboratories' representatives came and asked me whether I would be willing to conduct experiments with their unit. Always interested in anything new that might turn out to be of use or be beneficial, I readily agreed to participate in such trials. Too late, however, did I realize that in order to be able to include the Proportioner in my water lines, I had to run by-pass lines to it from the main supply line, and from it to each of the individual lines, and shutoffs in each to be able to manipulate the appropriate valves. It meant a lot of unanticipated work. A week of soldering copper pipe, tees, angles, couplings, fittings and valves together became a "Rube Goldberg" that looked and functioned so well that pictures of it even made it into some of the poultry press.

I finally had what I wanted: A farm operation as efficient as I could make it, dependable help that did not need continuous supervision, and enough eggs of a quality and quantity that could satisfy even the most demanding customers.

41.

Home Improvements

KAUFMAN'S POULTRY FARM'S buildings had been expanded and populated with as many chickens as possible and vertical integration of all activities had been accomplished over time without any hitches. I now had enough eggs to supply all the eggs the Fort Dix Commissary was using and ended up being its primary supplier most of the time. Every so often another egg dealer would have an egg shipment on the store shelves at competitive, usually cheaper prices, but the customers were the final authority and they stayed with the consistent exceptional quality product they had become used to.

A few years passed during which life on the farm went on without any problems. All the flocks had remained disease free; we had overcome the previous problem with the feed mixing, and the birds were producing as well as could reasonably be expected. Supply and demand for eggs were in balance, with an occasional surplus sent to a dealer. The markup of about 5 cents per dozen over wholesale market prices made it easy to reduce outstanding financial obligations. Occasional post cards from friends and relatives away on vacations telling us: "Having a good time, wish you were here" did heckle us; we had not had a vacation since we bought the farm. Except for an overnight stay In New Hampshire in 1961 to celebrate Lotte and Fred's 25th wedding anniversary, it would become 27 years until we could get away for more than a day at a time. As good as the help was with everyday chores, no one was ever competent enough to manage the daily operation without supervision, and that kept us both close to home. To compensate for the lack of opportunity to sometimes get away from the farm, we kept our domestic social calendar very full. There was hardly a week when there were not one or two dinner dates at either our house or some friends home, and frequent trips to Philadelphia for visits with family.

Renee graduated from High School at Moorestown Friends School in 1968 and was college-bound for Syracuse University. The only advice that we gave her, and later also to Karen, was to consider preparing for a profession with which she could make a living, should she ever be on her own. Having taken summer courses, Renee graduated "Magna Cum Laude" in less than three years' time with a Bachelor of Science degree in Speech Pathology. A Master's degree at Columbia University followed where, after completing a two year program in one year, her Major again was Speech Pathology, and a Minor was in Audiology. While at Columbia, she had interned at the Veterans Administration Hospital in Brooklyn, New York, and upon graduation she became a clinician on the staff of the VA hospital at East Orange, New Jersey. She moved into an apartment in New York, and from then on came home only to "visit." Living in New York, she was able to spend and enjoy time with Ann and Joe, who were always glad to see her, and who by then were called their "step-grandparents" by both girls.

A short time after Renee had left home for college we embarked on still another building project. This time it was for the sake of comfort and convenience. The very small dining room in our house had always been a problem, and made serving meals and even moving chairs difficult. The solution was to take two feet away from the kitchen area, do away with the enclosed stairway to the basement that was between dining room and kitchen, and replace it with a different access to the basement.

Bruce and his crew were called upon to dig out needed space, and then to build an addition outside the house, along the kitchen and dining room walls, for a stairway to the basement, wide enough to even handle large objects.. The original kitchen door to the outside was moved out far enough to give access to the stairs as well as to the outdoors, and an entrance into the basement was created by breaking a doorway opening through the original foundation wall of the house. When the job was finished, the dining room was then large enough to comfortably accommodate ten people at the table, with lots of room to move around it. A buffet was built into the wall that separated the dining room and the bathroom, making good use of a nook in that wall. Happy with the work done by the craftsmen, we attacked the bathroom. The old bathtub was replaced by a modern one. A noiseless or silent toilet and a new vanity cabinet and sink were in place after insulation material had been installed in the wall between the dining room and the bathroom. Next was a remodeling of the kitchen, where the cabinet makers built a utility and supply cabinet that Mina loved because it was exceptionally functional and practical. It became the envy of many a homemaker guest who saw it. Calls for "somebody" to come help do the dishes also ended shortly after Renee had left for college, when a new dishwasher became part of the renovation. Life in the house became a lot easier and more comfortable after all the changes had been made.

The well Milton had drilled was primarily for use in the poultry coop, and through a long buried pipeline it also supplied our home. There had always been the danger of the line freezing in winter, and it had happened several times to Milton. Feeling that this layout was inadequate and not safe enough, I decided to have a new well drilled next to the house. The well driller came and went to work, drilling for water. Foot after foot of four inch diameter pipe got pushed into the bored hole, and at 65 feet there was the first show of water, with little volume and a lot of sand in it. The drilling went on, and at 125 feet there was another stream of water that also was not strong enough, and not clean enough. Finally, after 225 feet of pipe had been rammed down into the hole, the drill hit an aquifer that brought up clear, alkaline water that, when tested, was found acceptable, potable and fit for human consumption. The drill had landed in a thick bed of sea shells—20 miles distant from the nearest point on the Atlantic Ocean!

Meanwhile, Karen was about to spend another year at the New Egypt School when Renee graduated at Moorestown Friends School. We gave her the choice of attending MFS a year earlier than her sister had done, or staying at the local school for one more year. Karen's choice was as expected, and she ended up coping with the same travel routine that had kept Renee in route to and from school for several hours each day. We wanted to make sure that Karen would have the same opportunity to attend a private school that we had given Renee. She adjusted well to the new environment, and in her junior year was class president. Loving animals—not especially the ones her parents made a living from—she spent a lot of weekends working for "Dr. Pete," a veterinarian in nearby Wrightstown, volunteering for whatever job he let her do. Like her father, she also wanted to become a veterinarian. After she graduated from High School, cum laude, she went to Michigan State University where they had a veterinary school. On leaving the house for the trip to East Lansing, as she was heading for the car that was loaded with all her gear, she turned wistfully and said: "I don't know why I am leaving. I am homesick already."

Karen was not at all happy at Michigan State. It was a large school that had a social climate she was not used to and, after the second trimester—the school had an accelerated program—her advisor told her, to her great disappointment, that she had no chance of being accepted into the professional school because Michigan had no reciprocity arrangement with New Jersey and he suggested that she choose a different course of action. Given that advice, and homesick as she was, Karen decided to transfer to a school closer to home at the end of the school year. She was accepted at Georgetown University in Washington, DC and elected to take courses that prepared her for a career in business. She was able to transfer all of her credits earned at Michigan State University, and, by taking summer courses, she also finished with a baccalaureate degree in three years' time. Hoping to go to Harvard University for a Master's Degree in Finance, she was told to get several years of work experience and then to reapply. New York University would give her full credit for any of the courses she had taken at Georgetown, but its rigorous program required two years attendance of everyone. To save her parents the extra expense, Karen ended up going to George Washington University in DC, part of a consortium to which Georgetown University also belongs. There she was given credit for required courses she had already taken, and where, after twelve months, she received her Master's Degree in Finance. During the time she was at GW, she also took some private lessons preparing for a CPA (Certified Public Accountant) exam. We knew when she sat for the exam, and, while standing in the candling booth that day, Mina received a two-word phone call: "I passed," and the phone went dead, end of call. Karen had passed the entire exam on her first attempt. After leaving GU quarters at St. Albans, she moved to a studio apartment close to "Five Corners," near the office of a CPA firm where she had interned until she graduated from GW. She pursued several job opportunities after that, staying in the Washington area. She also came just to "visit" from then on, but for both Renee and Karen home was always where their parents were. We had bought a used car for each of them after they graduated and had to commute to wherever they entered the working world. A lack of transportation for a "visit home" then also never became an issue.

The year 1977 provided a pleasant surprise for us. We were informed that the State Poultry Association had voted unanimously to award us the year's "Golden Egg" for "Meritorious Service to the Poultry Industry in New Jersey," the first time in its history the award was given to a husband and wife team. In January 1978 a banquet at Cedar Gardens in Mercerville that honored us and was attended by about 200 people that included Ann and Joe Blumenthal who braved a taxi ride from and back to New York on roads covered with several inches of snow, and Harry Fenton who flew in from Florida expressly to be present at his friends' big day. The citation describing the Kaufmans' achievements was read by John Bezpa, the Rutgers University Poultry Specialist, and the presentation of the award was made by Professor Dr. John Gerwig, Director of Rutgers Extension Service. I thanked the Association for selecting us for the honor, and I also thanked the Rutgers Poultry Department and Dick Hartman and Harry Fenton specifically for all the help they had been to us over the years. I singled out Ann and Joe for having saved my life, and Renee and Karen for always being ready to pitch in when needed. Needless to say, I also thanked everyone for having come to this award presentation, especially since snow had made travel very difficult that evening.

What could have turned into a terrible accident the day before the banquet had a fortunate ending. Renee was in her car on her way home from New York when, not far from Hightstown, at a bend in the road she tried to avoid an oncoming car and hit a patch of black ice, causing her to lose control. The car hit a bank on the side of the road, rolled over and landed upside down on the field next to the road. The car was "totaled," but a terrified Renee walked away from it—miraculously without a scratch. The seatbelt had saved her life. A phone call from a neighboring farmhouse had me anxiously rushing to pick her up, and a grateful family sat down to dinner that night.

42.

Empty Nesters

LIFE WITHOUT HAVING our children at home was not easy to get used to. We realized that we would become "empty nesters" when, following Renee's example, Karen with some help from home also bought and moved into a condominium apartment. Both girls had good jobs in their chosen professions and supported themselves. They made friends and created their own social circles. Mina and I were persuaded by Army friends to join their synagogue in Mt. Holly. Our interest was more social than religious, and over time we turned into quite active members. I served as Financial Secretary for seventeen years, and Mina was in charge of the kitchen and, with the help of other volunteers, often prepared dinners for the entire congregation or meals for special occasions.

The family Torah scroll that Mina had been able to save from destruction during the Holocaust and was able to bring to this country with her household goods, found a new home and was getting continuous use during services at Mt. Holly's Temple Har Zion. It had been in use at a temple in Philadelphia, where Menko family members attended services until that congregation merged with another synagogue, and its several sacred scrolls were distributed to other synagogues. Mina and I in time replaced the beautiful decorative silver ornaments that the Nazis had ordered stripped off when Mina took the Torah out of the Temple ark at Wuerzburg-Heidingsfeld, just a few hours before Crystal Night began on November 9, 1938 when the temple was burned to the ground.

Together with Bill and Dottie McDaniel we attended a Beginners Bridge course offered at the Mt. Holly High School. Unable to make that a foursome once the course was over, we were glad to find friends in New Egypt, Paul DeHaas and his wife Doris, who were willing to give novices at the game a chance to hone their skill. It became a once a week evening game that went on for a long time.

I had been asked by New Egypt's mayor to serve on the township's Planning Board and I chaired it for many years after Roger Atkinson resigned from the Board. When a vacancy occurred on the Ocean County Planning Board, I also became Plumsted's representative and stayed on that board for eight years. Meetings of the various agricultural organizations also took up some of my time. And after all, there was still the farm and business to take care of.

Much to our relief, by 1972 the "chickens' contributions" and a lot of hard work and worry during more than twenty years had helped us to pay off the mortgages on farm and home. The farm's routine had changed somewhat when after selling Kaufman's eggs for seventeen years the Sterling Davis Dairy went out of business. I was able to find a new steady customer who would take nearly as many cases of eggs as had been sold on the dairy's milk routes. The man had extensive retail egg routes and he picked up what he needed twice each week. Supply and demand therefore remained fairly in balance. The physical operation of the farm began taking up more of my time when after many years buildings and equipment showed signs of wear and tear.

Once we were free of debts and able to plan ahead, we decided to incorporate the farm, making Renee and Karen part owners and directors of the new "Kaufman Enterprises, Inc." They had willingly helped us whenever they could as long as they were home, and we felt that making them part owners with equal shares would be fair and could possibly simplify matters, should other people in the future become an influencing part in their lives. The incorporation also included the creation of pension plans for Mina and me, as well as for the company's full-time employees.

The Production Credit Association had a requirement that only an active borrower could be a director in its organization, and since I enjoyed the association and wanted to remain on the Board, I maintained a one hundred dollar loan balance. After almost 25 years I paid off the long carried "loan," and after I retired from the Board, both Mina and I kept up a close friendship with Ann Myles, who by that time had become the first female bank president in the National Federal Farm Credit system. For the first time since we had bought the farm, we finally had some money that was not already obligated and committed, and we acquired 32 shares of stock of the "First National Bank of New Egypt." Roger Atkinson, a director of the bank, had bought them for us when they were being auctioned off as part of an estate settlement. At last, being able to put some money away for the future and retirement was very comforting.

As to retirement, there was no way that Renee and Karen would ever think of returning home to operate the farm. Buildings and equipment were becoming or were already obsolete, and with our advancing age both of us had to think about retiring. We realized that with new residential housing going up ever closer to the farm, and with the distinct "birdy odor" emanating from the hen houses, it would be impossible to sell the farm as an ongoing operation. Phasing out would be the only solution. Little did we know how soon we would have to face a totally unexpected development that would have us considering just that as the next most important decision involving our business.

Kaufman's Poultry Farm had supplied the Fort Dix Army Commissary with eggs for more than thirteen years without ever getting a single complaint about price, quality or service, from store personnel, or anyone of several Commissary Officers who had succeeded each other. Suddenly, orders changing purchase procedures arrived at the Commissary Office, directing that when existing contracts ran out, local purchases of certain food items, eggs included, were to be discontinued. These purchases had originally been authorized to create good will, and to support the local economy. Offers to sell to military commissaries by qualified vendors—of which Kaufman's Poultry Farm was one—from then on had to be submitted in bid form on a quarterly basis to a Department of Defense procurement agency at Fort Meade, MD, with fixed prices quoted each time for a ninety day delivery period. Existing minimum quality standards that Kaufman's eggs had always exceeded by far became the accepted norm. While with local purchase the Vets were instructed to reject any shipment that did not contain eggs that met at least 80 % grade "A" quality, the new contract requirements soon permitted financial adjustments to be made for acceptance of shipments that the food inspectors previously would have rejected.

For an egg dealer who can adjust purchases to his supply and demand conditions fairly easily, a periodic bidding process does not present the problem that it does for an egg producer who does not have that choice. The dealer can change the volume of eggs he buys if he loses a contract and bid again three months later. A farmer who produces the eggs cannot afford to bid on a contract that he may be awarded for one three month period, and then lose it for the next. He needs a steady outlet.

Feeling that we could manage financially, Mina and I decided to give up the Fort Dix account, by far our largest customer. The new terms made being able to hold that account too uncertain since price, and not better quality, became the determining factor now in continuing to service the account. Not having a written contract, I kept on delivering eggs to the store at Fort Dix as long as I was able to. At the same time I stopped replacing all of our flocks when their production ceased to be profitable, thereby gradually emptying pens and buildings. For some time I had more eggs than my other customers needed and I sold them to a dealer. Then I arranged to get delivery of as many nest-run, unprocessed eggs as I needed from a farmer friend while our own farm's egg production dropped gradually and then stopped completely. Mina and her helpers washed, candled, graded and packed those nest-run eggs to our own farm's high quality standards, and we kept our remaining customers satisfied.

Once I began reducing our flocks, there was not enough work for the men who did the daily farm routine. Fortunately, I was able to find a job for Kenny at a turkey farm nearby, the owner of which also bought the feed truck and the feed mill. In fact, Kenny helped his new boss and some other men to dismantle the entire structure and he moved off with them. Harold and his family moved away as soon as he found a new job. Bill, the young local man who lived in the little house I had bought from Frank Myronchuck found another job and stayed on as a renter. With work reduced to two days a week and fewer hours in the packing plant, several of the young women of Mina's crew soon left for other jobs, and I began helping out when I was not making deliveries to some of our remaining customers. When for some reason I could not make deliveries myself, Dan Shelton, a retired US Air Force master sergeant who lived in the neighborhood was glad to earn spending money by making the deliveries for me.

All major car, tractor and truck maintenance had always been done for us by Jack Horner, of whom it was said that in a few hours he could make a tractor "purr like a kitten after having been buried in a swamp for a year." While I did almost all of the plumbing that needed doing on the farm, I had Bob Conk, the local licensed plumber do all the work on the upgrades in the family home. Raymond Grant was the electrician whom I could count on to do the more difficult electrical hookups for the feed mill and the emergency generators. The three men, Jack, Bob and Raymond were indispensable backups I could always depend on, day or night.

In 1979, after 27 long years of not having a single vacation, Mina and I were at last able to get away. There were no chickens to take care of, and work in the processing plant was easier since we did not have to put the eggs for our now biggest customer into individual dozen cartons, and there was little change in the weekly quantity of eggs our other customers used. During her years at home and often working with her parents, Renee was familiar with the plant's routine. She spent part of her 1979 annual vacation in New Egypt, handled egg processing and the business end of the activities while Dan made all deliveries, and we were off, to Israel. My sister Lotte, whose husband Fred had died several months earlier, was glad to travel with us.

I had been corresponding with two cousins who had also been lucky to get out of Germany, and I had not seen them since they left home. Both Noemi and her sister Ruth, daughters of my uncle Josef, my mother's only surviving brother, as 14 and 17 year olds in the nineteen-thirties had been able to go to Palestine with "Youth Aliyah," a Zionist youth organization. They participated in Israel's

1948 War of Independence, and after it ended they were gradually able to attain a more normal lifestyle. Noemi lived in Haifa and had married Perly Pelzig, an artist who is famous for having created new or restored historic ceramic tile monuments in Israel as well as in many other countries. Ruth and her husband Avram Loewy lived in Moledet, a "Moshav," that is primarily an agricultural settlement in which married couples had their own small house, and the unmarried people lived in a communal building. Avram was curator of the Natural History Museum at Ein Charod , and he seemed to know every square inch of land in Israel. It certainly appeared that way when, as a tour guide for us from Metulla on the Lebanese border to Eilat on the Red Sea, there was not a site with which he was not familiar, and the history of which he could not explain.

Needless to say, highpoints of the tour were visits to Jerusalem, the Western Wall, and to Yad Vashem, the Holocaust Memorial Museum. There, Lotte and I tried to find out if it had any records or any information that would shed light on our parents' fate. Only years later did we find out that our parents had been murdered in March 1942 at Belzec, a Death Camp in Poland. On the last day of our stay—Lotte was going to stay another week—Ruth made a farewell dinner for Mina and me, attended by all Loewy and Pelzig family members, young and old. Some were in military uniforms. It was not easy for the cousins to say good bye to each other at the airport, and promises were made for reciprocal visits—soon.

The flight home was exhausting, and we were glad to get back to our daily routine. Renee had taken care of business beautifully, and she was also glad to get back to her apartment in New York, her job in New Jersey and her friends. With spare time on our hands now, we took weekend and day trips, visiting friends and relatives, and doing some sightseeing. Quite often we spent weekends in West Cornwall, Connecticut, visiting Ann and Joe Blumenthal who had retired there. Not forgotten was "Bruno," the last one in a succession of dogs that had followed when Buster, the family's all-time favorite, had died at age eleven. Monsignor Griffin was a good friend and next door neighbor who had two Labrador Retrievers. Vera, his housekeeper, cooked food for their dogs every day while we always fed our dog "Kibbles," a dry commercial dog food. If one or the other of the neighbors was away for more than a day, whoever was home made sure that all three dogs got their food and water. It never failed that, when we came home after a day or two away and gave Bruno his dried dog food, he visibly snubbed us until he was hungry enough to eat his "plain" ration again.

A year later Lotte, Mina and I attended the 90th birthday party of my mother's cousin Felix Kaufmann, in Santa Barbara, CA, while Renee and Karen competently took care of their parent's chores and charges. Felix previously had worked as a clerk in a clothing store in New York until his 80th birthday, and never looked his age. He had surprised his disbelieving employer when he told him his age and that he was going to quit because he was "now old enough to retire and go on Social Security." Having enjoyed the celebration and the visit with Felix and his family, we three travelers went on to San Diego, visiting sites and attractions in and around the city for several days. Then we boarded a cruise ship that took us on a seven day voyage along the Mexican Riviera. Home looked very good when we got off the plane and were back in familiar settings. Even though we were glad to be back at home, the "traveling bug" had gotten hold of both of Mina and me, and another trip was soon to follow.

Bert Schweizer, on whose father's farm Peter, our first dog had spent his final years, lived with his wife Judy in Everett, near Amherst, MA, where Professor Bert taught math at the University of Massachusetts. During a summer vacation, he and Judy spent two weeks in New Egypt as our houseguests—while we, the hosts, were away. It gave the Schweizers an opportunity to visit friends and relatives in the area, but it also gave Bert a "job" to do: To oversee processing and delivering of eggs for ten days, most of which had been preplanned and prearranged. The three women in the processing plant and Dan were conscientious and could be depended upon. A day after Bert and Judy arrived, Mina and I were on our way again.

Lotte , Mina's sister Rosa, Mina and I got off the plane at Calgary, rented a car and were soon on our way to the Canadian Rockies. After two days of taking in the sights of Banff and its vicinity, the foursome had lunch at the beautiful Hotel Lake Louise, and also stopped briefly at Mirror Lake. After a restful night in Jasper, we woke up in the morning and were surprised by a big Elk with large antlers looking in on us at our open cabin window. The stay in Jasper was pleasant, and then it was back to Banff, to turn in the car and take the 24 hour train ride to Vancouver on the Canadian Railroad. Not having made reservations for cabins or compartments early enough, the four of us spent the train ride alternately moving from our seats in the passenger car to the dining car and the observation car, avoiding the rest rooms as much as possible. The train had begun its ride days earlier on Canada's east coast and care of the rest rooms was badly lacking. After arriving in Vancouver in the morning, and before moving on to Seattle, we took a ferry to Victoria and visited Butchart Gardens, 55 acres of beautiful flowers.

We had timed our arrival in Seattle perfectly and were just in time to attend the wedding of Carl Roer, the son of our cousin Fred, who had moved to Seattle from California in 1947, several years after arriving in this Country. An accomplished plumber, he had been trained in Germany and had been expected, together with his brother Hermann, to take over grandfather Gustav's business after their father was killed in that tragic trolley car accident in Cologne. He had survived the Holocaust because of his expertise that the Nazis took advantage of, but he was unable to join a union and get a job as a plumber in this country. He had been in charge of maintenance in a large warehouse until health problems he had contracted at Auschwitz became aggravated and he had to stop working. We were the only members of his father's family present at the wedding, where Rosa was also welcomed as "family." After the wedding and a day of sightseeing that included a ride up to the observation deck and lunch on the Space Needle, four happy campers boarded a plane for the flight home, the last leg of a great vacation.

Relieving Bert and really playing hosts to the Schweizers for a few days, we were glad that all had gone well in our absence. When I, as a matter of habit, went through the unlocked empty poultry buildings, I found that burglars had paid a visit and torn out all the copper water pipes and the electric wiring in every building. I immediately suspected someone in the neighborhood who I knew was doing drugs and might have sold the copper to feed his habit, but I had no way of proving it. After that discovery, and not seeing any possible future use for the empty buildings, and to eliminate temptations of curious trespassers to look around, I decided to do away with all four poultry houses. Soon a wrecking crew made short shrift of them as trucks hauled away the demolished parts. I also felt that not having useless buildings on the property might help to make a possible future sale more attractive to a potential buyer.

43.

Coasting

TONY WIKSWO WAS still alternately planting corn and soy beans on the crop field while I supplied seed and fertilizer, and we split the receipts. As long as the feed mill was in operation, I had always bought Tony's share of the corn he grew on our farm, in addition to what he grew on his own farm. He now sold all corn to the dealer to whom he had sold his soy beans all along. My sole job on the farm turned into keeping grass and weeds under control.

With substantially reduced business and more time on our hands, we were able to catch up and make use of the invitations we had received over the years when we were unable to get away. Not bothered by the stress of business, we also enjoyed having more time for each other.

On one of our trips out west Karen went along when she had a week's vacation. After seeing the Grand Canyon from above, in a six-passenger plane, and enjoying rides through several other national parks, we drove Karen to Reno for the flight back east. The Air Traffic Controllers had gone on strike during that time, and it took some "nail biting" and worrying until she was able to get a plane back to Washington. After seeing her off, we continued our sightseeing journey to the West Coast for another week.

There was little change in our farm's activities for quite some time since I had not solicited any new customers. Then one day Bob, the man who had the retail egg routes and who had bought the bulk of our eggs for several years told me that he was going out of business and retiring. When he left, I felt it was senseless to keep on processing the relatively few cases of eggs for which we still had customers. It was not worth keeping Mina and her helpers working for about three hours to process a week's needs, but I wanted to keep busy and active. I spoke to the farmer who had supplied me with nest-run eggs and arranged to get the eggs I now needed from him in already processed form, washed, candled and sized. I became an egg dealer. Having sold the big delivery truck, I was able to use my van to make the deliveries that were still well worth my time and effort in less than two days a week. Dan was familiar with the routes; he also had a key to the building and very often made deliveries for me. We were now able to get away from home much easier for a week or even longer periods. Shortly after we stopped running the machines in the plant, we took the women who had stayed on and the ones who had left earlier to a last Friday evening buffet dinner at the Cock & Bull restaurant in Lahaska, PA, something we had treated them to every year around Christmas.

With only the in-cooler or holding room still being used, and the grader and washer maintained in excellent condition, I was able to sell them, along with the big 35-Kw emergency power plant, to a farmer who had ducks as well as chickens and wanted to upgrade his operation. Once they were gone, the only piece of farm equipment I had not sold was a John Deere tractor with mower, front end loader and the scraper attachments that I used to mow the grass on the farm and to dig out our own and some neighbors' driveways when there was a lot of snow. I held on to it.

The weather was nice when late in 1984 Mina and I took a trip to England. It had always been one of Mina's hopes to get to London, with all its history, and its theatres. Distant cousins of hers, a family of 10, had settled there after fleeing Germany and were all killed in an air raid during WW II, when a bomb hit their shelter. For me it was revisiting places I had been to while I was in England before the invasion on D-day. There was Buckingham Palace to see, Westminster Abbey and the Tower of London as well as many other sights in and around London to visit. A side trip took us to the

Roman baths at Bath. In London and vicinity we used public transportation, while for longer trips we rented a car, and I had to re-learn to drive on the "other" side of the road. On the way to Bath we went through Warminster in the Salisbury Plain, where I had spent almost five months, living in an army barracks that was still there, unchanged. Stonehenge was not far from there. A rope surrounded the stones when we got there, and a guard told us that vandals had smeared grafitty on some of the monuments and that he was there to prevent further damage. When I told him that for some months during WW II I had been stationed at nearby Warminster and been to Stonehenge several times, he excitedly reached into a pocket and gave Mina what he said was a little piece of one of the stones, as a "token of thanks" to me for having helped defend his country. After admiring the well preserved Roman Baths in the town of Bath we returned to London, took a last stroll through Hyde Park and headed for the airport for the flight home, ending a trip that made Mina feel especially good.

Back home again, with a lot of time at her disposal, Mina joined a Hadassah Chapter, a Jewish women's charitable organization. I was being kept busy attending meetings of the various civic groups I belonged to that included the local Lions Club, AUSA, state and county agricultural groups and the township Planning Board that I chaired. Casinos had opened in Atlantic City, and I could not resist the temptation to "try my luck." Mina just went along. After our first visit, we went occasionally to "visit our money," as I called it, making sure that I never exceeded the limit of my hard earned money I was going to "donate" for my fun. The more than fifteen theatre performances we saw together with the McDaniel's each year always included dinner either before or after the shows. Social life had become our primary pastime, and we gradually got used to it.

Although the egg route and rent from the houses and the bungalow on the farm took care of most of our living expenses, we decided the time had come to sell the farm and to get rid of its responsibility and the maintenance it required. Real Estate prices had also appreciated considerably during the 34 years that we had owned the farm. We had its value appraised, set a price and listed it with a broker. There seemed to be no immediate interest, nothing that made us stay at home.

We had often talked about it, and when in June 1985 Renee and Karen both were able to take vacations at the same time, we took them to Germany, to the places where our families had lived and where we had grown up. We also went to the beaches of Normandy in France, where I had landed on Omaha Beach in June of 1944. When we arrived at the airport at Luxemburg, we rented a car and headed south, to Germany, through the Eifel Mountains towards Drove, my birthplace. We drove past the cemetery at Bitburg that President Reagen had honored with a wreath laying, much against objections raised in three separate resolutions introduced in Congress, and many individual communications sent to the White House. The objections had been raised because, along with regular German soldiers, SS men were buried there who might have been involved in some of the many atrocities committed by the SS during the war. The objections included a letter from me that Representative James Saxton hand-carried to Washington, promising that it would get delivered to the President's office. There was no response.

In Drove we were received by Johann Richter, an architect with whom I had corresponded, and whom I had asked to order and arrange for the erection of two monuments at the Jewish cemetery. One had been placed at the grave of my grandfather Gustav who had died in June of 1941 and who I thought was the last person buried at the cemetery. The Nazis would not permit that he be moved and buried next to grandmother Caroline in the Jewish cemetery at Kerpen, some 20 miles away. My parents most likely were not able to or allowed to order a gravestone for him. It turned out that the monument I had ordered had been placed at the grave of another person who I did not know had come to Drove and who died there after Grandfather. Needless to say, feeling disturbed and sad, I had the monument moved from the one unmarked grave to the other one where Grandfather Gustav actually lies.

The other monument I had asked to be erected on a vacant spot at the cemetery. The inscription on it simply states that it was dedicated to the memory of my deported parents Leo and Else Kaufmann and (my father's aunt) Johanna (Hannchen) Kaufmann. Near it was a monument erected by the townspeople of Drove, in memory of all its Jewish citizens who had become victims of the Nazis. They had also placed a monument and a plaque at the site where the synagogue once stood, now just an empty space, overgrown with bushes and some flowers.

A nice young couple who lived in the house I was born in permitted us to go through it, while I pointed out how things were arranged when I had lived there. The house had remained undamaged during the war and not much of it had been changed since then. It had been rented out after my parents, and Lotte and I moved across the street in 1930, when 72 year old Aunt Hannchen did not feel comfortable any more with just her and the maid living in the big five bedroom house. Invited into the "house across the street" in which I had lived until I left for the U.S., and from which my parents were deported in March of 1942, I noted that the artistic new owner had made a few changes. The butcher shop and all the outbuildings had been destroyed during the war, but the garden and the several acres of pasture next to the house with all the different fruit trees were still as I remembered them. I had sold the house to Johann Richter's daughter when our farm desperately needed an infusion of cash. The young woman had lived in this country, in California, for several years, spoke English and took over explaining to Renee and Karen whatever she knew about the house and the town's history since the war. There was one woman whom I just had to visit and to thank. It was 86 year old Mathilda Klinkenberg, who for almost all of her life had been the maid in a Jewish family's home. I had been told that during the years of the Nazi regime she had openly and publicly defied them, but she was never arrested. When her employers were evicted from their home in 1941, and when with all the other Jewish families of Drove they were herded into my family's house, from where they all were then deported, she almost daily managed to bring some donated food to the many people confined there. She had not seen me for more than 45 years, but she still remembered me, bitterly lamenting what had been done to "all those good Jews" in town.

From the hotel in Dueren, where we stayed during the next part of our journey, we drove over newly constructed highways to Nideggen, a town in which we visited the ruins of an old medieval castle. The area around the "Burg" had been developed into a favorite excursion destination because of its location. It had been built in the 15th century, and the view into the valleys around it was exceptionally beautiful. At a millennium celebration at the castle in 1928, the antique oil lamp that generations of Kaufmanns had lit on Friday nights to invoke the Sabbath was one of the items on display. Disassembled, I was able to pack it into my luggage and bring it to this country where, held up by a wall bracket that I had made, it now decorates our living room. Interesting to all of us was a trip to the Schwammenauel Dam. It and the Urft Talsperre, another dam upstream on the Roer River, were the subjects of the important German military studies that I had found during the war. In them the Germans had calculated what would happen if both dams were blown. The dam had been completely rebuilt and was holding back a large body of water, a lake on which now a lot of pleasure boats were sailing. The evening was topped off with dinner at the home of Anni Kroll, an old Elementary School friend of mine who lived in Nideggen, and with whom I had stayed in touch since the end of the war. Her husband Werner had been in the German Army during WW II, was captured by the Russians and had not been released by them until 1950. He arrived home five years after the war had ended.

The next day we drove to Langenbroich, a town not far from the Belgian border, for a visit with Nobel Laureate Heinrich Boell and his wife. He had corresponded with me before he wrote his article *Die Juden von Drove* (The Jews of Drove) in the book titled *Koeln und das Rheinische Judentum* (Cologne and Jewish presence along the Rhine), and was glad to be able to discuss the article with me. Mr. Boell's political views were not very popular with many people at the time, and he said that he had purposely moved from Cologne to a village close to the Belgian Border because he had received threats to his life. The time spent with the Boells was very animated and much too short. Mr. Boell was very interested in hearing what my life had been like after leaving Germany, what Renee and Karen were doing, and what their interests were. We were only let go after promising to come back once more for a visit the next day, which we gladly did.

Another short visit to Drove for a few more photographs, and we were headed for Buir, where my grandparents had lived and where my mother, and also Lotte had been born. The house had been damaged during the war, but its newly painted front still looked the way I remembered it. A few pictures were taken and the next stop was at the cemetery at Kerpen, where Grandmother Caroline and her sons Felix and Karl were interred, and where my grandfather Gustav had also wanted to be buried. Then it was on to Cologne for an overnight stay. A city tour included the "Dom," the famous medieval cathedral. Allied bombers during the war must have been ordered to specifically avoid hitting it during heavy air raids on the city, because it had not sustained any damage at all. Very interesting was a tour of the German- Roman Museum, where exhibits pictured a very active Roman presence in the city before the Common Era.

On the way to Wuerzburg we took a scenic road along the Rhine River, passing where remnants of the Remagen Bridge stood and a plaque on a wall described how American troops had been able to establish a beachhead across the river and move across it in force before the Germans were able to destroy it. The girls marveled at the pretty landscape along the river and the many vineyards; they saw the Lorelei and many attractive villages. When we got closer to Frankfurt, I made a side-trip to Oberursel, to "Camp King," the "Headquarters, European Command Intelligence Center" at the time I was stationed there in 1947/48. By 1985 the camp had become the headquarters of a U.S. Army transportation unit. When I showed my Military Identification card (that I carry as a retiree) and told an astonished guard that I had been stationed at the camp nearly 40 years ago, I was allowed to drive in. I headed for what used to be the Officers Club and saw that it had become the mess hall for all troops. What flabbergasted all four of us was that, when I walked into the dining room with my family, a civilian showed up and said to me "I remember you. You were a major when you were here." That the baldheaded waiter, whom everybody at ECIC used to call "Curly" was still there, and could remember and recognize anyone that far back left me speechless! The man was even able to recall the names of some officers who served with me at the same time. Camp King had changed, and not much of interest was there for the two girls to see. An hour later Wuerzburg- Heidingsfeld, a suburb of Wuerzburg, came into view, and it did not take long for us to check in at the hotel where we intended to stay for several days.

The first trip the next morning was to house "Klosterstrasse 4," directly across from where the original Menko family home used to stand—it had been destroyed during the war—to the house in which the younger Menko family members had lived as tenants until they left for the U.S. Otto Beck, whose parents had been good landlords and friends of Mina's family, excitedly explained what had happened to the building since the last time Mina had seen it. War damage had been repaired and on the ground floor his wife Helga was busy running a very nice "Beck's Cheese Wares" store, selling cheeses, cold cuts, sweets, alcohol and delicacies. Otto had arranged to get the key to the Jewish cemetery, which was locked since there had not been any more burials in over 40 years, and he knew that Mina wanted to visit her father's grave. Her father had died in 1929, and his grave could only be recognized by the white marble plate with his name on it at the base of the stone. The weather had done its damage to all the stones. With all four of us trying, there was little chance of finding the graves of Mina's paternal grand and great grandparents who were also buried in the hundreds of years-old cemetery, but Renee was lucky. She found the grave of her paternal great-grandmother (her namesake) with the name still spelled "Mengo."

After the visit at the cemetery, Mina relished the thought of being able to show her family the places she used to frequent as a teenager in Wuerzburg, except, she could not find them anymore. Bombed during the war, the entire old city had been destroyed and had since been rebuilt. The old landmarks she remembered had disappeared. The "Residenz," the Bishop's Palace that is the city's main attraction, had survived with little damage, and walking through it everyone had to marvel at the frescoes beautifully painted by Tiepolo, the famous Venetian artist. Walking around Fortress Marienburg provided a great panoramic view of the entire city and the bridge across the Main

River. Dinner that evening was with Otto and Helga Beck, and the fare of delicacies was provided from their store. The next day the tourists drove to Rothenburg o/d Tauber, the only city in Germany whose medieval city wall and fortifications were still completely intact. Then followed a visit to Eubigheim, some distance away, with a visit to the cemetery where Mina's maternal grandparents were buried. On our last day in Mina's old hometown Otto and Helga took us to the Rhoen Mountains, to an area next to the East-West German Border. The sight was eerie. A high fence separated a heavily trafficked West side from a desolate East side from which watch towers overlooked the territory. "No Trespassing" and "Stop - Border" signs were posted all around, warning people to stay away from the fence. After a short farewell at the Becks the following morning, our car traveled west, heading for Normandy in France. Doing some more sightseeing on the way, and after an overnight stay in Heidelberg, we soon crossed the border into France, when both Renee and Karen commented that they were "castled-out" and "cathedraled-out," and were anxious to get to where we were headed next.

A non-stop ride, bypassing the typical roadside pit stops and Versailles got us to the Chateau Du Molay, a Best Western Hotel at Littry, near Bayeux. Using the hotel as a base, we first drove to the vicinity of Isigny, a village near the sector of the coast that had been named "Omaha Beach" during the invasion, and where I had come ashore. From an observation platform we saw a perfectly smooth, waveless ocean and a clean beach that belied the murderous fighting that had taken place there. As we walked on the beach and looked in the opposite direction, the view changed drastically. There was Pointe du Hoc, the cliff that an American Ranger Battalion was able to secure, and with its feat helped to make the landing a success. We next visited the American Military Cemetery at St. Laurent Sur Mere, an awe inspiring place, where over 9,000 American soldiers had been buried; a number reduced from many thousands more who were repatriated after first having been interred there. A day was spent retracing where the 113th Cavalry Group had gone into action, with my team attached to it. We drove through St. Lo, which still showed signs of war damage. One of the most impressive places we visited in Normandy was the monastery at Mont St. Michel which was built in 709 on a rock that even 45 feet high tides have not been able to wash away. We had saved for last a trip to Bayeux, to see the Bayeux Tapestries. These tapestries were made around 1070 on a piece of linen 230 feet long, with about 50 scenes embroidered on them with colored woolen yarn. The scenes were depicting events that led up to the Norman conquest of England, and were so impressive that they caused "some" in my family to talk about hitting history books to refresh their memory once they got home.

All four Kaufmans prepared to leave idyllic Chateau du Molay, and they hated to leave its delicious French cuisine. The girls' vacations were ending, and the trip was becoming a cherished memory. On the way to Luxemburg, from where we were to fly home, we stopped at Rheims to look at the windows that Marc Chagall had been asked to do at the cathedral. From there we visited one last cemetery—the American Military Cemetery at Hamm, near Luxemburg, where General Patton is buried. A short city tour and one last night at a hotel in Luxemburg, where we "killed" a bottle of wine that Otto Beck had given us when we left Wuerzburg – Heidingsfeld. I had kept it in my luggage during the entire trip. A sentimental journey that would often be talked about in the future ended with an uneventful flight home.

44.

Selling the Farm

NOTHING OF IMPORTANCE had happened while we were away. Bruno howled and kept jumping up on us as soon as we opened the door to his run, and Monsignor Griffin had again kept a watchful neighborly eye on our house. He was anxious to hear us tell him and his sister, "Sister Helen" about our trip. Sister Helen had come from her Order's Motherhouse in Brooklyn to visit him. Dan had done well taking care of the egg customers, and as before, it was quickly back to the usual activities—but not quite.

John Begley, a local real estate salesman told me that he had a client looking for a property suitable for a horse farm, and he was wondering if Kaufman's farm was for sale. The agency I had dealt with previously had not come up with a single interested person over quite some time, and when John showed interest, I was ready to listen. He soon came to us with a couple who were looking for a farm on which they could keep horses that they were planning to race at the Freehold Track. They had sold an apartment building in New York and were ready to move to the country and buy a farm. After walking around the farm with John and looking at its houses and the bungalow, they came across the road to introduce themselves and to talk to Mina and me. They immediately fell in love with the house that they walked into and offered, if a deal could be made, to buy both the farm and the house at the same time. We told them we were just not ready to sell our house. I suggested to them that, at least on a temporary basis, they could live in one of the homes on the farm, and as soon as they wanted to, they could build a new house to suit their taste. When I told them about the egg business that was well worth the time and effort, they said they would not mind continuing it. I had given John my asking price for the farm, and it did not seem to be much out of line and it kept them interested. They wanted time to think it over. It took a few weeks until John called and said that the couple was back in his office, ready to buy the farm, but had a condition and some questions they first wanted to discuss. While sitting in our dining room over a cup of coffee and some of Mina's cake, the contract was worked out. The condition was that the egg business and van be included in the asking price. The first of the questions was whether or not they could move into one of the houses on the farm a short time before the final settlement, with John holding a sizable down payment in escrow. The second question was whether I would continue the egg business until they were settled in and could take over, and the last one was whether we would be willing to hold a mortgage. Since we had done an extensive Title Search when we bought the farm and there were no mortgages to satisfy or other financial obligations to meet, we saw no problem with what had been asked. We were satisfied with the down payment, were also willing to assume a mortgage at a reasonable rate of interest, and we signed the contract. Final settlement was at the end of December and we started 1986 "farmless." How much easier it was to sell the farm than it had been to buy it 35 years earlier, when we were about to become "homeless."

I had kept my customers supplied for as long as I had been asked to, telling them that the new owners of my farm would continue to serve them. Within a few days however, after the new owners were to have made their first weekly delivery, I received frantic phone calls from exasperated customers who wanted to know when they would get their eggs. Apologetically, I could only tell them that I had not been told by the new owners of their decision not to bother with selling eggs, and I suggested to all of them that they look for a new supplier. We had made ourselves available to the new owners for whatever help we could be to them, but we never found out why that part of the arrangement had not been kept. Shortly after spring weather permitted, I saw movement on the level part of the farm on which crops had been raised, and I was told that a training track for horses was being laid out. No other activity seemed to take place for quite some time after that.

Since we were now able to just lock the door and have the dog cared for by Vera, Maurice Griffin's housekeeper, we made up for a lot of lost vacation time. In addition to one day outings, there were flights for three day stays to Bermuda, to the Bahamas, and to Las Vegas. There were some overnight trips to Atlantic City, where we kept on "visiting" our money. And there were the frequent theatre performances to which we traveled with the McDaniels. Both Renee and Karen were doing well, and we enjoyed being completely re-tired. In 1987 we visited Israel again, with the travel arrangements being somewhat unusual. As a military retiree and along with my "dependent" Mina we were entitled to free "space available" flights on military airplanes wherever they went. It meant going to a Military Airbase, carrying one's own luggage, and waiting around for a sched-uled or unscheduled outgoing flight that could take passengers along. If flights, usually cargo planes, had any space available, passengers were taken on according to their place on a list of categories, with active duty personnel being first and retirees being last. If planes were carrying hazardous cargo or inclement weather was expected, it was the pilot's option to refuse to take unessential passengers on board. With our luggage in the trunk of the car, we left our locked home and drove to McGuire Air Force base, six miles away. We parked our car and went to the Terminal Building, where we found out that the only flight that was going out that day was to a base in England, and that it was fully loaded and could not take passengers. There were no other outgoing flights. We went home, spent the night and hoped to catch a flight the next day. A similar situation presented itself that day. A flight going to Rhine/Main Airbase in Germany took on some uniformed active duty soldiers who were returning to their duty stations from leave, which left us and some other would be travelers outranked. We drove home again, left our luggage in the trunk of the car and hoped for better luck the next day. On the third day at the Terminal we were told that a DC 10, a big civilian plane, had been chartered by the Air

Force and was leaving in the evening from Philadelphia to a Persian Gulf destination, would stopover at Aviano Airbase in Italy, and that there would be quite a number of seats available. After driving home once again I immediately called Dan who was able to drive us to the Philadelphia Airport. Less than half of the huge airplane was occupied when it took off, with us and all other passengers enjoying comfortable seats. We were even being treated to a box type supper. At the Terminal at McGuire I had seen a list of many scheduled flights from different military airports, and on it was an Embassy Supply flight, a C-130 that was to leave the next day from Aviano for Lod Airport in Israel, which happened to be our hoped for eventual destination.

Spending a night at the guesthouse after arriving at Aviano Airbase, we two adventurers were seated next to each other on canvas seats along the fuselage of the turbo prop plane that took off as scheduled the next morning. Using earplugs that we had been given by a crew member, we conversed by passing notes to each other during the more than three hours long, noisy flight. After our arrival at Lod Airport and exiting with the plane crew through the airport's strict security system without being checked, I quickly found a phone and called Avram, my cousin Ruth's husband. After waiting for about an hour I was able to load our valpacks into his car. With Avram and Ruth, to whom we had only given an approximate arrival time once we landed at Aviano, we soon were on our way to Moledet for what turned into a week-long visit. After the exchange of family news, plans were made for a family get-together and then the four of us were off, sightseeing, with Avram taking us to places we had not seen during previous visits.

We were having a great time, but after about a week I made a phone call to Haifa, where several American warships were based, to inquire about return flights. I spoke to someone who was able to tell me that once a week a C-130 flew from Lod to Athens, and usually had some sailors going on leave on board. He stated that there would be several empty seats on the next day's flight. Not wanting to miss out on that opportunity, and also not prepared to stay another week, we quickly decided. There followed several short goodbye visits. Some plans were cancelled, and Ruth and Avram took us to the airport the next morning. We could not have picked the timing of our trip home any better because, when we landed in Athens, we found out that a chartered DC 10 airplane on a return trip to Philadelphia from the Gulf area was due to land there the next afternoon. It would be on the runway for a short time, and only a very few seats on it might be available. The night was spent at a guesthouse on the base, and after breakfast at the Air Force mess, we waited for "our" plane's arrival. It came as scheduled, and when it departed, we had been cleared to board and were lucky to find two seats in the just about fully loaded plane. Fortunately, there had been no other "space available" travelers competing with us for seats. The plane made another stop at Rota Airbase in Spain, long enough to give its passengers a chance to get out for a short time and stretch their legs before it headed over the Atlantic Ocean. We arrived in Philadelphia at 3:30 AM, and were finally close to home. Travel expenses for the entire trip were $25 for Airport Taxes, and $50 for the taxi ride home from the Philadelphia airport.

Life was comfortable and casual for quite some time. We enjoyed entertaining, had a busy social calendar and an occasional weekend or longer getaway. We had enjoyed our "space available" trip so much that we soon thereafter took another one. One late April day we had no trouble at all catching a C-141 cargo plane at McGuire AFB that would carry some passengers and went to Frankfurt, Germany. The weather forecast was not too encouraging, but we hoped it would change for the better once we were in Germany. Our plan was to rent a car and drive to where tulips were just coming into bloom in Holland. When we arrived in Frankfurt, icy rain greeted us, the temperature was below 40 degrees and forecasts were for much the same cool and rainy weather also in Holland for the next five days. Not having made any other plans, we simply decided to turn around and fly home again. We were stuck in the passenger terminal at Rhine/Main Airport for over 24 hours before one of a number of planes that were leaving for the States had space for us. On arriving back home, we both agreed that the next time we were going to fly, we would not drag our luggage around or sweat over when and to where we could catch a flight.

From then on it would only be civilian airlines with definite destinations and scheduled departures and arrivals.

Although we were now retired, I was still interested in the activities at the farm. For several months I did not see anything happening. There was no movement at all, and the new owners were often away for days. I was surprised, but did not ask any questions when either of them came to our house asking for some advice, or to simply sit and talk for a while, with good natured Mina serving up her usual cup of coffee and cake. Then, one morning the woman came running over to us, crying, and told us that someone had taken a shot at her in the house while her husband was away. She declared that she was not going to stay in the house any more. It turned out that her husband had left her and had returned to his homeland in Europe where he still had a family. Police investigation did not turn up anything that substantiated her story, and after that she left her house to stay with friends, leaving the farm unattended. When the monthly mortgage payments suddenly stopped, I contacted the couple's lawyer and was told that the farm had been sold to a local builder, and that within a few weeks the mortgage and the overdue monthly payments would be paid in full. We received all the money that was due us, and never saw the husband or his wife again. Within two years 40 single family homes stood on what had been Kaufman's Poultry Farm that was supposed to have become a horse farm.

Sadly, our neighbor Msgr. Griffin had died and Sister Helen only occasionally came to spend a few days at her "Retreat," and that stopped when travel for her became physically difficult. Many of the people we knew at Ft. Dix and were friendly with had moved, been retired or transferred to other Military Posts. Except for recently widowed Paul DeHaas and the Atkinsons, we had not established many social contacts with people in New Egypt. We had made friends in Mt. Holly after we had joined Temple Har Zion, and most of our relatives lived in the Philadelphia area. We had frequent visits from Renee and Karen and a lot of other casual traffic, but we were beginning to feel physically isolated. We were bored because of the lack of structured activities, and we felt that we were too far away from those we cared about. Bruno, our last dog had developed hip dysplasia, a disease that crippled him so much that he could barely move. I had to take him to a veterinarian to be euthanized. Much as we loved the dogs we had for all those years, there would not be another one because we were planning on traveling a lot, and it would be unfair to an animal to be left alone for longer periods of time. And travel we did. We took Cruises in the Caribbean, from Valparaiso in Chile around Cape Horn in South America, a Scandinavian cruise to the Baltic Capitals, the Norwegian Fjords, the Eastern Mediterranean, and also several more flights to Israel for visits with Noemi, Ruth and Avram, who by then had also been our guests in this Country. But knowing that we could also take cruises and other trips if we lived somewhere else, and considering our advanced age, moving to a continuing care type adult community was something we thought about. When we talked about it with our children, we were encouraged by them both saying: "We love our house in New Egypt, but our home is wherever you are. It would be the biggest gift you could give us, because we would worry less about you, knowing that you were no longer living in such an isolated place."

We were proud of our children. Renee had become head of the combined Speech and Hearing Sections at the Veterans Hospital where she was employed. Karen was V.P. Finance and Controller of a company large enough to be listed on the N.Y. Stock Exchange. At a simple civil ceremony she had become the wife of Robert Yin, a PhD in Experimental Psychology who was the owner of Cosmos Corporation, a social sciences "Think Tank." At the Willard Hotel in Washington they hosted more than one hundred guests and celebrated their union in style. Three years later Karen presented our family with a new member. Andrew was born on October 15, 1992, lively and healthy. As soon as she was able to, Karen returned to her job, having an "au pair" take care of her son while she was at work. Andrew grew up nicely, and whenever he and his parents visited us, one of his greatest pleasures was sitting on the tractor with me when I took him for rides. I was glad that I had kept the big John Deere tractor with its attachments when I sold the farm, because, in addition to snow removal, it came in handy for grounds maintenance on the more than ten acres of land that surrounded our house.

During all the years since I arrived in New York in 1939, I had always stayed in close touch with Ann and Joe, who, after living in New York for many years, had permanently moved to what used to be their summer home in West Cornwall, Connecticut. We were always glad to visit them whenever it suited them. The conversations were always lovely and lively, covering a great many subjects, and Joe and I on occasion had opposite opinions about the state of the world. When one winter Joe called and mentioned that they had been without electricity and shivered through several days, I thought about how loving and generous Joe and Ann had been when Mina and I were facing terrible times; I ordered an emergency generator to be shipped to them. When I was informed that it had arrived, we took Raymond Grant, our local licensed electrician and his wife with us on a visit to West Cornwall. When we went home, the generator had been installed and was in running condition, big enough to alternately heat the house, keep the refrigerator temperature where it should be, or power the water pump.

For a long time nearly 93 year old Joe had been complaining about back pain and insomnia. At our last visit, when I was telling him what farm and time and especially his and Ann's generosity had done for us financially, Joe casually said to me that he hoped I would not mind being the executor of his will. I of course felt honored, proud that Joe had so much trust and confidence in me. Not long after that visit we had a call from Ken Keskinen, a friend and neighbor of Joe and Ann's. Joe had asked him to come to their house the next morning and said that the door would be unlocked. When Ken went to the house in the morning, wondering what Joe wanted, he found both of them lying lifeless in their beds. They had died during the night. Letters addressed to six people, one of them to me, were on a table nearby. Mine was a loving farewell letter that terribly upset and saddened all four of us, and even I could not keep tears away. It was close family we had lost. In the letter Joe mentioned that he had changed his will, had made Ken the executor of it when he realized that it would involve considerable time and a lot of travel for me to settle his matters, and that he knew I would understand. We had long known that Joe and Ann belonged to the

Hemlock Society, wanted to stay together, and never wanted to go to a nursing home.

Mina and I were both close to 80 years old when we finally decided to sell the house. It had been fourteen years since we sold the farm, and kept the house. We now wanted to move to a place where we would not have to maintain a house and worry about the grounds around it. I called John Begley and told him what we intended to do and asked him to put the house on the market. With not even a "nibble" for a while, John felt that the asking price was too high and he suggested that we lower it somewhat. As soon as we had reduced the asking price a bit, John had two parties who were interested. A young couple asked permission to go through the house and was not heard from any more, but the other one, a builder, was more interested in the land and did not even bother to inspect the house. He was immediately ready to negotiate and close a deal. He had calculated that the property had enough acreage for seven houses to be built on it in addition to the existing one, and that its location was ideal, since a lot of it was fronting on the highway. He was ready to settle for a price that I finally had quoted and said he could close the deal if we were willing to accept a reasonable down-payment and hold the mortgage for the balance. He explained that he had several houses under construction at the moment; his money was tied up in them, and he was not sure he could get bank financing for the purchase. As consideration we could stay in the house for up to two years by just paying real estate taxes, utilities and keeping the house in its present condition. He would also buy the tractor that he could use in his business.

Sad as we were about leaving the only home we really called our own and had loved and lived in for forty years, conditions of the sale could not have been better for us. The down payment and the mortgage secured our interest, and we had two years during which to look for the right place to move to. Our old friend Ann Myles had told us that she was on a waiting list for admission to Medford Leas, a not-for-profit Quaker oriented non-denominational Continuing Care Adult Retirement Community, and that she would move there after she retired. The waiting list was nine years long and it was unlikely that, not being on that list, moving to Medford Leas would be possible for us. To find out what to expect if we moved to a CCRC, we visited several existing ones. Some were for profit, and some were not. We compared what each offered and what joining would cost. We talked to some residents and heard differing opinions about care and treatment at their communities, depending on what each of them considered important. Living as inexpensively as we did in our own home and having plenty of time before we had to make up our minds, there was no need to make hasty decisions. We took our time and got away from home some more, this time for two weeks. We went on a bus tour of America's National Parks that started with a flight to Rapid City, South Dakota, and ended 2,400 miles later with a flight home from Denver, Colorado. Both of us said later that the tour was unforgettably beautiful, educational and exciting, and called it the best trip of all the ones we had ever taken.

Word got around that Medford Leas was expanding and building a satellite community in Lumberton, five miles away from its main campus, for seniors who were able to live independently. We found out from friends that the prevailing waiting list had been exhausted, and that Medford Leas was offering access to its health care facilities to its Lumberton Leas residents, either by a "partial care" contract or by "fees for service" care. That was exactly what we were looking for, and after visiting a home at the Lumberton site, whose occupants graciously showed us around their house and told us about amenities and activities in their community, we went directly to the administration office at Medford Leas in Medford.

At Medford Leas we were told about the community's various activities and given a tour of buildings and facilities. We admired the well maintained grounds that were connected with the University of Pennsylvania's arboretum. Expressing serious interest, we were taken back to Lumberton Leas and shown which houses or sites for one, two or three bedroom units were still available. Given diagrams of building layouts, a list of available options, a sample residence contract to study, and told of the financial requirements and monthly maintenance payments that had to be met, it took a few days for us to make up our minds. We could not think of any major disadvantages. Within easy travel distance for both daughters, and close proximity to Philadelphia, even the location appealed to us. We decided to buy in and signed a contract for "Partial Care" that would give us lifelong residence and all the health care we would ever need. If and when a physical or mental condition required, we would be moved to Assisted Living, Nursing or other care facilities at the Medford Leas campus. We picked a two bedroom house at a site where up to that time only basement and foundation walls had been poured. We asked for a few minor options to be included in the construction, and were told that the house would be finished and ready for occupancy in about six weeks. With the open-ended arrangement about staying in our house in New Egypt, the timing for the move worked out very well. There was ample time to send out change-of-address notices, to cancel utilities and to notify whoever had to be notified. As projected, on April 17, 2001, 129 Woodside Drive in Lumberton was ready for occupancy. A moving van took all our large items to our new abode. As soon as the van was unloaded, its contents in places intended for them, and the mover's crew gone, the house became our new home.

It did not take long for us to settle in and meet our new neighbors. Mina loved her big kitchen and soon was back at what she had always loved to do: prepare meals and host dinners for friends and relatives. The County Library was not far away, and weekly visits had her pick up and "devour" three or four books each week, while I no longer had to worry about lawns that needed mowing, or driveways that needed plowing when it snowed.

Realizing that the number of Holocaust survivors and World War II veterans was shrinking continuously, that their number was getting smaller all the time, and fewer people were left who could relate what they personally experienced during the horrible years of the Nazi regime and WW II, I had followed Navy Captain John Ingraham's admonition and was always ready to speak at schools or to any groups or organizations that wanted to hear my story. I joined the speaker roster of the Holocaust Memorial and Education Center at the Jewish Community Campus at Cherry Hill, NJ. I was going to tell my story as long as I was able to do so. People should "Never forget."

During this time, family, friends and our newfound freedom was accentuated. Getting together with our children and grandson was always our greatest pleasure, and there were new friends to exchange visits with, more cruises, tours and trips to be taken, and there was always the computer which I loved, or an invitation to a Bridge game for both of us. Mina and I were content and thankful that we were able to enjoy this kind of life together in retirement.

And as long as I live, I will always remember that, when in May, 1939 I left home and said good bye to my parents, whom I would never see again because they were murdered in the Holocaust, my father's last words to me had been:

"Don't do anything I'd have to be ashamed of."

In retrospect, I think my father would not have had to worry.

CPSIA information can be obtained
at www.ICGtesting.com
Printed in the USA
LVOW08s2008150517

534583LV00004B/692/P